BEHAVIOR

An RTI
Approach
for Nurturing
Essential
Life Skills

Behavior: THE FORGOTTEN CURRICULUM

*MSEC
ND BEHAVIORAL GRANT 23 - 24
Grand Forks Public Schools*

Chris Weber

Solution Tree | Press

a division of
Solution Tree

555 North Morton Street
Bloomington, IN 47404
800.733.6786 (toll free) / 812.336.7700
FAX: 812.336.7790

email: info@SolutionTree.com
SolutionTree.com

Visit **go.SolutionTree.com/RTI** to download the free reproducibles in this book.

Printed in the United States of America

Library of Congress Cataloging-in-Publication Data

Names: Weber, Chris (Chris A.), author.

Title: Behavior : the forgotten curriculum : an RTI approach for nurturing essential life skills / Chris Weber.

Description: Bloomington, IN : Solution Tree Press, [2018] | Includes bibliographical references and index.

Identifiers: LCCN 2017049055 | ISBN 9781943874323 (perfect bound)

Subjects: LCSH: Problem children--Education--United States. | Behavior disorders in children--United States. | Response to intervention (Learning disabled children)--United States. | Academic achievement--Psychological aspects. | Behavioral assessment of children. | Metacognition in children. | Behavior modification.

Classification: LCC LC4802 .W43 2018 | DDC 371.93--dc23 LC record available at https://lccn.loc.gov/2017049055

Solution Tree

Jeffrey C. Jones, CEO
Edmund M. Ackerman, President

Solution Tree Press

President and Publisher: Douglas M. Rife
Editorial Director: Sarah Payne-Mills
Art Director: Rian Anderson
Managing Production Editor: Kendra Slayton
Production Editor: Alissa Voss
Senior Editor: Amy Rubenstein
Copy Editor: Ashante K. Thomas
Proofreader: Elisabeth Abrams
Cover Designer: Rian Anderson

Acknowledgments

As an author, consultant, and educator, there is no better partner than Solution Tree. Guided by Jeff Jones, Solution Tree is the preeminent educational publishing and professional development company in the world. There is no finer man or publisher than Solution Tree Press president and publisher, Douglas Rife, and I thank him for a decade of support. Thanks to Alissa Voss for her outstanding support in editing this book; no one supports an author in creating a book better than Solution Tree. I must thank the professional development and events departments at Solution Tree, led by Shannon Ritz and Renee Marshall, for supporting me and others as we share our passion and ideas with colleagues around the world. I hope this book moves Solution Tree one step closer to achieving their vision of transforming education worldwide. The systematic behavior supports described in this book are grounded squarely in the research of positive behavior interventions and supports (PBIS). George Sugai and Rob Horner, guiding lights in PBIS, have made such a significant and positive impact on schools. While I did not collaborate directly with these researchers on this book, I thank them for their collective contributions to our profession. Thanks to my friends, coauthors, and colleagues Mike Mattos, Austin Buffum, Janet Malone, and Laurie Robinson Sammons for guiding me so patiently and wisely in my professional journey. Finally, I believe that Rick DuFour was the most innovative, transformational, and significant educator in the United States since Benjamin Bloom; I miss him and honor his work. There is no response to intervention (RTI), multi-tiered system of support (MTSS), or positive behavior interventions and supports (PBIS) without the foundations of Professional Learning Communities at Work®. Along with Bob Eaker, Becky DuFour, and PLC at Work® associates, I look forward to a day when PLCs are not something we do, but simply who we are.

Solution Tree Press would like to thank the following reviewers:

Margaret Adams
Assistant Superintendent for Teaching and Learning
Melrose Public Schools
Melrose, Massachusetts

Hailey Lehman
Regional Behavior Specialist
Rochester, New York

Louis Lim
Vice Principal
Bayview Secondary School
Richmond Hill, Ontario
Canada

Nancy Moradi
Positive Behavioral Interventions and Supports Coach
San Jose Unified School District
San Jose, California

Lucy Worthington
Response to Intervention Coordinator/
  Behavior Specialist
Jeff Davis County Schools
Hazlehurst, Georgia

Visit **go.SolutionTree.com/RTI** to download the free reproducibles in this book.

Table of Contents

About the Author

Chris Weber, EdD, is an expert in behavior, mathematics, and response to intervention (RTI) who consults and presents internationally to audiences on important topics in education. As a teacher, principal, and director in California and Illinois, Chris and his colleagues developed RTI systems that have led to high levels of learning at schools across the United States.

In addition to writing and consulting, he continues to work in Irvine Unified School District in California, supporting some of the best and highest-performing schools in the country.

Chris has been in service to community and country his entire life. A graduate of the U.S. Air Force Academy, he flew C-141s during his military career. He is also a former high school, middle school, and elementary school teacher and administrator.

To learn more about Chris's work, visit Chris Weber Education (http://chriswebereducation.com) or follow @WeberEducation on Twitter.

To book Chris Weber for professional development, contact pd@SolutionTree.com.

Introduction

Jacob is a fourth-grade student in an urban school district. After losing his mom three years earlier, Jacob, his older brother, and younger sister now live in a single-parent home. Their father works two jobs to take care of the family, but he doesn't earn enough wages to pay all the family's living expenses. Jacob's aunt often cares for him and his siblings along with her three younger children. Some days, Jacob's aunt asks the older children to watch the younger children. Jacob's role as caregiver means he often makes his brother, sister, and cousins breakfast, helps them get dressed, organizes their lunches and backpacks, and walks them to their classrooms. Jacob is sometimes late to his own class or absent on these mornings.

Jacob and his siblings have witnessed varying degrees of violence and drug use in the community. His dad's work demands make it hard to have routines, like a set bedtime or homework time. Jacob and his siblings sometimes don't have meals at home. Jacob is often hungry but feels ashamed to ask for extra food at school, while watching other students waste theirs.

Despite these traumas, Jacob likes school. Jacob enjoys numbers and logic puzzles and has experienced success in mathematics. He has good peer relationships and generally fits in well in classes. When he is attentive, his teachers remark that he is a good contributor and can be seen smiling. When he is not, his teachers become concerned about the impact of Jacob's inattentiveness on his learning and of his disruptions on others' learning. When Jacob becomes frustrated, he lashes out verbally, and occasionally, physically. Staff recognize that detentions and other negative consequences that have been assigned are having little impact but don't know of other strategies. They want a consistent approach for all students, and not separate rules for Jacob. Jacob's father is busy and has a difficult time committing to school appointments, but when his father has met with staff, he has expressed his respect and support for a good education. He wants a better life for Jacob and his other children.

Jacob wishes his teachers knew that school is important to him. His realities outside of school make it challenging for him to always manage, monitor, and regulate his behaviors. He's often hungry and tired. He tries to push through these feelings, but it doesn't always work. His absences and tardies are increasingly contributing to difficulties.

Jacob's situation is, unfortunately, not unique. There are many, many students in the North American school system facing familial and financial challenges just like Jacob's—and students with needs that are slightly less dramatic are even more common. In fact, over half of U.S. students live in poverty (Suitts, 2015). Jacob's story provides critically important context for the causes—loss of a parent, economic struggles, food scarcity, violence, or lack of structure at home—behind what many teachers may simply pass off as troublesome classroom behavior. We should continue to strive for classroom environments in which students are engaged and attentive, complete the work assigned to them, and demonstrate clear progress at the end of the unit compared with the beginning. The truth is, many students around North America experience difficulties displaying such behaviors because their life situations have presented challenges in mastering these skills. When home, health, and hunger are unreliable variables, successful self-regulation may vary too. Let's continue to expect and recommit to teach and support, and let's do so with empathy.

Students are inherently and intrinsically creative and curious, but they also long for safe and predictable environments that allow them chances to develop such skills as exercising autonomy, practicing independence, demonstrating competence, growing in learning, and forming relationships and connections (Ryan & Deci, 2000). These behavioral skills foster complex thinking and social-emotional growth (Denton, 2005), which lead to success not only in classrooms but also in life.

All students deserve that we, as educators, nurture their behavioral skills as well as their academic skills. Doing so should not be difficult—both sets of skills require students to learn problem solving, metacognition, and critical thinking, so there should be some degree of overlap in what is taught. However, in an attempt to cover the increasing number of academic state standards and ensure our students are compliant, we have lost sight of our responsibility to consider our students' fundamental behavioral needs—those skills that form the foundation of an education and a life.

I passionately believe that the most important instructional and behavioral principles and practices for students—differentiation, growth mindset, self-assessment, metacognition, and perseverance, to name a few—are inextricably related. Research finds that these skills are mutually reinforcing concepts that will improve student engagement, nurture noncognitive skills, and lead to greater academic performance (see, for example, Farrington et al., 2012). Instruction in one behavioral skill should positively affect the development of other skills, serving overall to improve school, career, and life outcomes for students.

This book builds on a research-based model of instruction and supports that is already familiar to educators—response to intervention, or RTI. This introduction presents to educators what RTI can be, should be, and truly is—the *what* and *why* of RTI, and how it applies to behavioral instruction. It defines behavioral skills and discusses the need for behavioral supports for *all* students—not just those displaying contrary behavior—since behavioral skills are necessary for any student to be successful in school, college, career, and life. It helps educators apply the latest information from research studies on behavior and its impacts on success to skills they can teach in their classrooms. Finally, it encourages readers to embrace the notion that behavioral skill development is a critical part of the educational experience and that each and every student has the capacity to learn and display positive behavioral skills. As stakeholders in the school community, educators, including administrators, should ensure that their learning spaces reflect an appreciation for and knowledge of behavioral skills, such that students in their classrooms view school as a welcoming environment that teaches, models, and nurtures behavioral skills.

Introducing Behavioral RTI

While educators have appreciated the importance of student behaviors as a necessary foundation on which to complete the "real work" of academics, many now recognize that behavioral skills are as important as, and perhaps more important than, academic skills. Whether we label behavioral skills as noncognitive skills, self-regulation, executive functioning, social-emotional learning, or more specifically as grit, self-control, or social intelligence, student mastery of these behavioral skills better predicts success in school, college, and life than test scores and measures of intellectual ability (Borghans, Golsteyn, Heckman, & Humphries, 2016; Duckworth, Quinn, & Tsukayama, 2012; Duckworth & Seligman, 2005; Heckman & Kautz, 2012; Noftle & Robins, 2007; Poropat, 2009). We as educators must collectively embrace this reality and better nurture these skills within our students. But how? The simplest solution is simply to take what we've already been doing with academics and apply the same process to behavior.

One of the most common models for teaching academic skills to students—all students—is RTI. According to RTI experts Austin Buffum, Mike Mattos, Chris Weber, and Tom Hierck (2015):

> RTI is a systematic process of tiered support to ensure every student receives the additional time and support needed to learn at high levels. RTI's underlying premise is that schools should not delay providing help for struggling students until they fall far enough behind to qualify for special education, but instead should provide timely, targeted, systematic interventions to all students who demonstrate the need (Buffum et al., 2012). Traditionally, the RTI process is represented in the shape of a pyramid. (p. 8)

Buffum and colleagues (2015) offer an illustration of that pyramid (figure I.1, page 4) and go on to explain its components:

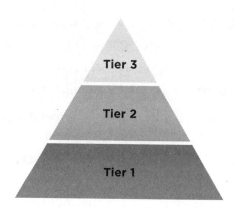

Source: Buffum et al., 2015, p. 8.

Figure I.1: The RTI pyramid.

The pyramid shape is wide at the bottom to represent the basic instruction that all students receive. As students demonstrate the need for additional support, they move up the pyramid, receiving increasingly more targeted and intensive help. Fewer students should need the services offered at the upper levels, thus creating the tapered shape of a pyramid. The pyramid is also traditionally separated into tiers, with Tier 1 representing grade-level core instruction, Tier 2 supplemental interventions, and Tier 3 intensive student support.

. . . RTI does not endorse or dictate a specific curriculum, assessment product, or intervention program, but instead creates processes that empower educators to make these critical decisions based on the specific learning needs of their students. While RTI processes are applicable to behavior interventions, RTI implementation efforts have traditionally focused on academic curriculum and instructional practices (Sugai, 2001). (p. 9)

Its process is applicable to behavior interventions. Response to intervention is a research-based set of practices. RTI plans are required within school districts in the United States, and most districts, schools, and educators are familiar with the principles and practices of RTI. Let's apply the familiar processes that we have applied to academics to the critically important area of behavioral skills.

The Six Steps of Behavioral RTI

Based on extensive research and empirical evidence, RTI is one of the most impactful sets of principles and practices in which schools can engage (Allington, 2011; Bloom, 1968, 1974, 1984; Burns, Appleton, & Stehouwer, 2005; Burns & Symington, 2002; Elbaum, Vaughn, Hughes, & Moody, 2000; Gersten, Beckmann, et al., 2009; Gersten, Compton, et al., 2009; Hattie, 2012; Swanson & Sachse-Lee, 2000; VanDerHeyden, Witt, & Gilbertson, 2007). However, in many schools, educators are applying RTI incorrectly, complicating the process, or misunderstanding the point entirely by focusing only on Tiers 2 and 3. Educators can follow certain steps, or elements, when applying the RTI model to alleviate these complications.

In behavioral RTI, district and school teachers and staff complete the following six core steps.

1.   Identify the most critical behavioral skills.

2.   Define and make sense of these skills.

3.   Model, teach, and nurture these skills.

4.   Measure student success in displaying these skills.

5.   Provide differentiated supports that respect students' current levels of readiness.

6.   Intervene appropriately and as necessary when evidence reveals the need.

These six essential steps to developing students' behavioral skills are the very same things that we do (or should do) as we strive to help students develop academic skills. Aligning our efforts and initiatives related to academics and behaviors is likely to decrease anxieties and increase efficacies.

This six-step behavioral RTI process ensures that a system exists for *predicting* and *preventing* frustration instead of reacting to students' behavioral deficits. For example, we can predict students will bring very different, identifiable behavioral needs to our classrooms. We can prevent frustration and delay by being ready to model, teach, and measure these behaviors. We can predict that students will need differentiated supports to successfully access and demonstrate mastery of essential behavioral concepts and skills; we can proactively and positively prepare with varied teaching and learning options for Tier 1. We can predict that some students will learn at different rates and will need more than our first, best instruction; we can then prepare with more time and alternative differentiated supports at regular, planned intervals for students in Tier 2. We can predict that some students will have significant deficits in foundational skills; we can then prepare immediate, intensive, and targeted supports for those in Tier 3. In essence, RTI is actively and systematically anticipating students' behavioral needs and proactively preparing supports. When we implement the six steps of behavioral RTI correctly, we serve students in a more timely, targeted, and organized manner.

RTI is a self-correcting system. When students are not responding to instruction and intervention, educators following RTI are ready with processes that ensure adjustments to their practices will be made until all students are responding and performing at or above grade level. Timely adjustments to supports are possible when applying the preceding six steps to the teaching and learning of behavioral skills.

For this six-step process to be impactful, RTI must be understood as applying to all students and embraced as the responsibility of all staff. Collective responsibility is a must. When all teachers and teacher teams are working together to apply the steps of behavioral RTI, it can become an effective system of teaching positive and necessary behavioral skills to all students in our classrooms.

Teacher Teams in Behavioral RTI

There is no RTI—whether in support or academic or behavioral skills—without Professional Learning Communities at Work®. RTI can be accurately described as "PLC+." In a PLC at Work, educators believe that a learning (not teaching) is the point of our supports for students; they believe that evidence-informed results, not opinions, must define the efficacy of our efforts; and they believe that the only way to meet our lofty and important goal of high levels of learning for all students is to work and serve students in collaborative teams (DuFour, DuFour, Eaker, Many, & Mattos, 2016).

The four critical questions of PLCs, which are embedded within the preceding six-step process, are well known to most educators (DuFour et al., 2016):

1. What do we want students to learn?

2. How will we know if they have learned it?

3. What will we do if they don't learn it?

4. How will we extend the learning for students who are already proficient?

Throughout *Behavior: The Forgotten Curriculum; An RTI Approach for Nurturing Essential Life Skills*, the tools, resources, and guidance provided are aimed at teacher teams working to provide behavioral RTI supports to students within the context of a PLC at Work.

Positive Behavior Interventions and Supports

Many educators interested in teaching behaviors may already be familiar with positive behavior interventions and supports (PBIS) and wonder why this book is focusing on RTI. In truth, a key goal of this book is to combine the elements of both RTI and PBIS. RTI has traditionally focused on proactively preparing and providing targeted supports in a collaborative, organized manner to meet the needs of different students, while PBIS has traditionally focused on the proactive and consistent modeling, reinforcing, and teaching of the behavioral skills that result in productive and positive environments. Both RTI and PBIS necessitate a schoolwide approach, and both provide different levels (tiers) of support to match the types and intensity of student needs.

Throughout this book, we work to incorporate up-to-date research on mindsets, social-emotional learning, and academic behaviors into RTI and PBIS to make them better integrated and more responsive to student needs, because, of course, different students have different behavioral needs. Students' beliefs about their ability to learn, and their levels of engagement and feelings of belonging, all influence how they act. One of this book's primary goals is to guide students' development of more productive behaviors. But which behaviors, both social and academic, are most critical to success? How do we determine which students need which kind of emotional and behavioral supports, and then how do we nurture those behaviors for all students? This book steps you through a process of definition, diagnosis, differentiated implementation, assessment, and culture building to move beyond simple behavior change to building learning dispositions to last students a lifetime.

Defining Behavioral Skills

Up until this point, this book has spoken rather generally about *behavioral skills*. But what skills exactly does that phrase entail? The work of Camille Farrington, senior research associate at the University of Chicago Consortium on School Research, and her colleagues (2012) influenced my definition of *behavioral skills*. Farrington et al.'s (2012) research-based framework describes six interrelated categories of behavior—(1) precognitive self-regulation, (2) mindsets, (3) social skills, (4) learning strategies, (5) perseverance, and (6) academic behaviors—all of which interact and influence student learning (academic performance). Figure I.2 shows the interconnectedness of these categories. Please note that the arrows flow in both directions. While positive mindsets foundationally impact positive social skills and learning strategies, which foundationally impact positive perseverance, which foundationally impacts positive academic behaviors and performance, influences can travel in the opposite direction. For example, difficulties with employing learning strategies can negatively impact a student's mindset.

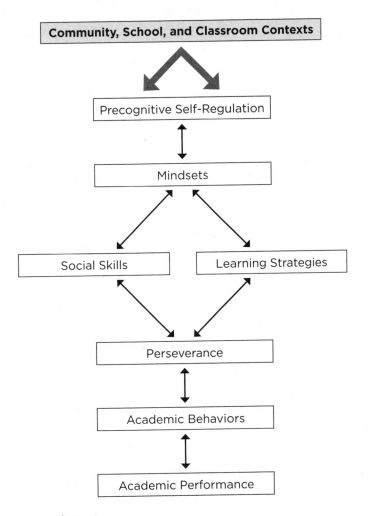

Source: Adapted from Farrington et al., 2012.

Figure I.2: Interrelated categories of behavior.

Farrington et al.'s (2012) categories fall under the umbrella of *noncognitive* factors. I prefer to think of them as *metacognitive skills* because everything in the brain is cognitive. The behaviors commonly associated with metacognitive skills include everything from attention and focus to grit and perseverance to empathy and engagement. Far from being noncognitive, these behaviors are considered part of the brain's executive functioning (Duckworth & Carlson, 2013; Dweck, Walton, & Cohen, 2014; Martens & Meller, 1990; Tough, 2012, 2016). Executive functions are processes that have to do with managing oneself (for example, emotions, thinking, and schedules) and one's resources (for example, notes, supports, and environments) in order to be successful. The term, in many ways, captures the preceding categories and may be considered as synonymous with the behavioral skills that we describe in the book and that students need to learn to succeed in school, college, career, and life. Each of Farrington et al.'s (2012) six categories contains what this book defines under the broad label of *behavioral skills*. Let's define the behaviors within each category individually.

1. **Precognitive self-regulation:** Students can attain, maintain, regulate, and change their level of arousal for a task or situation. Educators may observe that students have difficulty coping emotionally and may determine that these difficulties are impacted by poor health, nutrition, and sleep; or lack of exercise; or sensitivity to sensory inputs; or an ability to process inputs. These abilities are dependent on, and related to, physiological and safety needs as defined within Maslow's (1943, 1954) five-tiered theory of motivation.

2. **Mindsets:** Students feel a sense of belonging, belief, and engagement. Affirmative responses to the following statements represent a positive, growth mindset—

   - "I belong in this academic community." Educators know that students are connected to someone and something within the school environment.

   - "My ability and competence grow with my effort." Educators observe that students believe that they can improve with effort; that smart is something that you become, not something that you are.

   - "I can succeed at this." Educators know that success breeds success and that meeting students where they are and nudging them toward greater levels of proficiency are key; students draw on a sense of self-efficacy to persist in learning.

   - "This work has value for me." Educators know that motivation is dependent on the relevance that students see in classrooms; students have opportunities to explore passions, they see the purpose in learning, and they experience personalized supports and opportunities for personalized paths.

3. **Social skills:** Students have respectful interactions with others and demonstrate respect for themselves. Educators observe students cooperating and collaborating in socially appropriate ways and behaving with empathy for others in both academic and social circumstances.

4. **Learning strategies:** Students can regulate, monitor, and reflect on their learning. Educators see students employing effective study and organizational skills, behaving metacognitively, tracking their own progress, and responding appropriately when faced with a task, whether the task is completing an in-class assignment, completing a long-term project, or preparing for a test. Learning strategies can be thought of as cognitive self-regulation: students regulate the level of their learning frequently and make the necessary adjustments.

5. **Perseverance:** Students maintain effort and adapt to setbacks; they exercise self-discipline and self-control; they delay gratification; and they advocate for one's needs. Educators observe that students stick with tasks, typically because they are drawing on positive mindsets, social skills, and learning strategies.

6. **Academic behaviors:** Students are physically, emotionally, and cognitively present and attentive within learning and learning environments. Educators note that students consistently complete tasks of high quality; that they actively participate in learning; and that they appear motivated to learn, succeed, and grow. Again, educators' observations of academic behaviors

typically draw on and depend on positive mindsets, social skills, learning strategies, and perseverance, the companion behavioral skills in figure I.2 (page 7).

Defining behavioral skills within the context of Farrington et al.'s (2012) framework is helpful because the framework then becomes an action plan. We can operationalize the research, putting the best thinking of these experts into action and proactively supporting students in developing skills when difficulties exist. For example, let's say a student is labeled as unmotivated—he or she doesn't seem to care about school or his or her grades, or his or her future. This is perhaps the most common concern that educators identify, particularly as students get older. A lack of motivation would appear as a deficit in the category of *academic behaviors* within the framework. While we will describe how we can teach students to behave in more motivated ways, the sequential nature of the framework reveals that there are predictable antecedents to poor academic behaviors, or more specifically, a lack of motivation.

Considering the framework from top to bottom, a student who is hungry, is tired, has difficulties modulating emotions, or has some combination of these, may appear unmotivated, and more immediately, may not display positive, growth mindsets. A student without positive, growth mindsets may appear unmotivated, and more immediately, may not display positive social skills. A lack of social skills makes cooperating and collaborating with adults and students a challenge. Additionally, a student without positive, growth mindsets may not see the point or the payoff in practicing and improving learning strategies. A student without productive learning strategies may appear unmotivated, and more immediately, may not regularly persevere. Finally, a student who does not persevere will likely appear unmotivated. Essentially, the point of these examples is to illustrate that there are reasons—explanations, causes, antecedents—to a student's lack of motivation. When we as educators consider behavioral skills within the context of Farrington et al.'s (2012) framework, we can identify these reasons and do something about it. As John Seita (2014), associate professor of social work at Michigan State University, says, "Behavior is a form of communication providing clues about what is missing in a young person's life" (p. 29).

Identifying the Importance of Behavioral Skills

Research suggests that metacognitive behavioral skills matter a lot to students' long-term life success. For example, a long-term analysis of subjects from Walter Mischel's (2014) famous marshmallow study shows that children with strong self-regulation skills (who were able to resist the temptation of eating a second marshmallow) had greater academic and life success than their less strong-willed peers. Research further suggests that executive functioning and self-regulation are better predictors of school success than intelligence tests. (See Duckworth and Carlson, 2013, for one review of this research.) Education economist David Deming (2015) reveals that skill knowledge mastery and empathy—in this case, the ability to work with others to solve complex problems—are the critical combination for high-value jobs in the workplace. While definitions and tools for monitoring these learning characteristics are still emerging (for example, the Collaborative for Academic, Social, and Emotional Learning [www.casel.org], or CASEL, is working with a consortium of states to define common objectives), we should start incorporating them into our mix of measures now (Collaborative for Academic, Social, and Emotional Learning, 2018).

Despite the research indicating the importance of behavioral skills to life, the literature indicates that student readiness is lower than ever. While graduation rates are at an all-time high, ACT (2012) reports that less than 40 percent of students are ready for college. Why might this be? One possible explanation, revealed through an examination of the Lexile levels of texts, shows that while the complexity of text required in college, skilled careers, and the military has steadily increased, the text complexities within K–12 have not similarly increased. Another explanation is that the K–12 curriculum continues to be a mile wide and an inch deep—the curriculum covers a lot of material but doesn't examine it in depth.

It is my belief, and the belief of other pioneers of behavioral RTI, that a particularly significant explanation is that educators have not sufficiently focused on developing behavioral skills (Boynton & Boynton, 2005; Mullet, 2014; Sprick, Borgmeier, & Nolet, 2002; Sugai, 2001; Sugai & Horner, 2002; Walton & Cohen, 2011; Zimmerman, Bandura, & Martinez-Pons, 1992). We as educators may teach academic skills, but we have not prioritized the development of behavioral, or noncognitive, skills to the same extent. And to be clear, behavioral skills matter.

Several research studies investigating readiness for college and career paths indicate that behavioral preparedness is as important as, if not more so than, academics. The Partnership for 21st Century Learning (2016) organizes next-generation skills into the following ten categories.

1. Creativity and innovation
2. Critical thinking and problem solving
3. Communication and collaboration
4. Information and media literacy
5. Technological literacy
6. Flexibility and adaptability
7. Initiative and self-direction
8. Social and cross-cultural skills
9. Productivity and accountability
10. Leadership and responsibility

The skills within these categories are all more behavioral (or metacognitive) than academic. However, very few of these are explicitly taught by educators. It seems clear that these skills must be more prioritized within the work of classrooms and schools.

Further, David Conley's (2014) research investigates college- and career-readiness skills. His research, drawn from analyses of the skills required by colleges and careers, as well as the skills that students leave high schools possessing, led to his development of a framework for necessary 21st century learning. Among his findings are that the skills required for college and skilled careers are no longer distinct; success in either college or a skilled career requires the same competencies. Conley (2014) defines four categories of these skills, which table I.1 summarizes.

A simple analysis of these skills reveals the following: only one of the categories, Know, relates to academic knowledge. The other three categories define self-regulatory skills, metacognitive skills, and executive skills; in other words, the behavioral skills that were defined earlier in this introduction. This review of Conley's (2014) categories of college and career readiness leads to an undeniable conclusion: success in life is about more than academic knowledge. Behaviors matter, both in college and in the workplace.

TABLE I.1: FOUR CATEGORIES OF COLLEGE- AND CAREER-READINESS SKILLS

Skill Category	Definition
1. Think	Beyond retaining and applying, students process, manipulate, assemble, reassemble, examine, question, look for patterns, organize, and present. Students develop and employ strategies for problem solving when encountering a challenge. Strategies include: • Problem formulation • Research • Interpretation • Communication • Precision and accuracy
2. Know	Students possess foundational knowledge in core academic subjects and an understanding of: • Connections and structures between and within subjects • The necessity for, and implications of, effort and a growth mindset • The organization of content • Identification of key ideas • The inherent value of learning
3. Act	Students employ skills and techniques to enable them to exercise agency and ownership as they successfully manage their learning. Students gain expertise through the regular and integrated application and practice of key learning skills and techniques. Agency rests on the following: • Goal setting • Persistence • Self-awareness • Motivation • Self-advocacy • Progress monitoring • Self-efficacy Students develop habits that allow them to succeed in demanding situations: • Time management • Study skills • Test taking and note taking • Memorization • Strategic reading • Collaborative learning • Technological proficiencies
4. Go	Students preparing for a career or additional education develop skills to navigate potential challenges, including: • Contextual—Motivations and options for educational programs after high school • Procedural—The logistics of admissions and application processes • Financial—The costs of further education and financial aid options • Cultural—Differences between cultural norms in school and the workplace or postsecondary settings • Interpersonal—Advocating for oneself in complex situations

Source: Adapted from Conley, 2014.

The Economist Group and Google's (Tabary, 2015) survey of business executives to assess the skills workers most need in 21st century workplaces reinforces this reality. The ten skills they identify most are:

1. Problem solving (50 percent)
2. Team working (35 percent)
3. Communication (32 percent)
4. Critical thinking (27 percent)
5. Creativity (21 percent)
6. Leadership (18 percent)
7. Literacy (17 percent)
8. Digital literacy (16 percent)
9. Foreign language ability (15 percent)
10. Emotional intelligence (12 percent)

These skills are critical in all content areas and across all grades. They are not, however, sufficiently present within academic curricula.

Finally, research from the Hamilton Project and the Brookings Institution analyzed data from the National Longitudinal Survey of Youth 1979, with cognitive skills measured by the Armed Forces Qualification Test and noncognitive skills measured by the Rotter Locus of Control scale, the Rosenberg Self-Esteem scale, and Deming's (2015) social skills index. These multiple measures were compiled to measure attitudes about work and reward, self-esteem, and general social skills. The research drew the following seven conclusions.

1. The U.S. economy is demanding more noncognitive skills.
2. There are strong labor-market payoffs to both cognitive and noncognitive skills.
3. The labor market is increasingly rewarding noncognitive skills.
4. Those in the bottom quartile of noncognitive skills are only about one-third as likely to complete a postsecondary degree as are those in the top quartile.
5. Noncognitive skill development interventions improve student achievement and reduce behavior-related problems.
6. Preschool interventions emphasizing cognitive and noncognitive skill development have long-term economic benefits for participants.
7. A teacher's ability to improve noncognitive skills has more effect on graduation rates than does his or her ability to raise test scores.

The conclusions of this research are clear: noncognitive skills matter during and after a student's schooling, and behavioral skills are as important as academic skills. Research confirms that behavioral skills are the product of the interaction between students and educational contexts, rather than being predetermined characteristics of individual students (Deci, 1992; Ericsson & Pool, 2016; Farrington et al., 2012; Hattie, Biggs, & Purdie, 1996; Masten & Coatsworth, 1998; Stipek, 1988; Wang, Haertel, & Wahlberg, 1994; Yair, 2000).

Student behavior is neither innate nor fixed. We as educators can influence student behaviors—and we must. Many of the preceding studies aim to identify skills students need to develop now for use in the future. Because society and systems are continually evolving, it's difficult to pinpoint exactly what the schools of the future will look like. In many ways, we're in the process of retrofitting our schools, enhancing established structures with new principles and practices. As we continually question better ways of doing things, implement those ideas, and reflect on evidence of student success, more students will leave high schools ready for college and a skilled career. Schools will continue down a path of more innovation, inquiry, and integration of concepts, ideas, and processes. They will continue to find new ways of blending academic learning, behavioral skill development, and authentic student engagement into a rich and meaningful experience. Education holds the greatest promise to positively impact students' futures, and we as educators must be inspired to fulfill this promise. It is my hope that *Behavior: The Forgotten Curriculum; An RTI Approach for Nurturing Essential Life Skills* will support schools' continuous improvements.

In This Book

Behavior: The Forgotten Curriculum; An RTI Approach for Nurturing Essential Life Skills provides practical assistance, ideas, and resources for K–12 educators, administrators, teacher teams, and educational leaders as they strive to help students develop behavioral skills and self-regulation, with the ultimate goal of achieving better student outcomes. It provides administrators and teacher teams with both background and practical knowledge about how to design and implement comprehensive, RTI-based behavioral supports within their schools. Teachers who read this book on their own will gain insights into the most recent research in the area of behavioral skills and the best practices that they can use in their classrooms. Throughout the book, you'll also learn from educators—some researchers, some practitioners—who are pioneering behavioral RTI across North America and making the ideas presented within this book come to life.

This book is a *doing* book, chock-full of templates and tools for staff. There is a great need for behavioral supports for students, and an equally great need to build the capacities of staff to support student needs. As educators, we are simply less well-equipped and prepared to support students' behavioral needs and to help students develop mastery of critical behavioral skills than we are to support their academic needs. If best student outcomes are to occur, educators need to develop skills in teaching and supporting learning behaviors—and that is exactly what the tools in this book aim to do.

Chapter 1 provides tools for assessing your staff's readiness for behavioral RTI before introducing readers to the first two steps of the behavioral RTI model—identifying and defining and making sense of behavioral skill priorities. This chapter emphasizes the power of high expectations, the importance of proactively preparing supports, and the need to plan for core behavioral curricula in the same ways that we educators plan for academic units. After first discussing the collaborative culture of commitment and foundational beliefs required to implement behavioral RTI in schools and providing tools to measure such mindsets in staff, chapter 1 then provides tools to identify and define key essential student behaviors and describes how educators can establish both overarching and content-area-specific curricula to prepare them for consistently, comprehensively, and explicitly teaching these critical behavioral skills.

Next, chapter 2 delves into the effective modeling, teaching, and nurturing of behavioral skills within a Tier 1 environment. Within this chapter, readers will find a compelling rationale and specific suggestions for screening students; explicitly and comprehensively modeling, instructing, and reinforcing specific behaviors within the classroom; and nurturing these skills through supportive teacher-student relationships. Just as we incorporate sound instructional pedagogies and high-yield strategies for academics, we must apply sound instructional design to the learning of behavioral skills.

Chapter 3 focuses on assessment, differentiation, and intervention. It provides examples of formative assessments teachers can use to gather evidence of student success in displaying positive and productive behavioral skills, allowing educators to analyze performances, provide immediate and specific feedback, provide differentiated supports, and intervene appropriately, when necessary.

Anticipating that some students will need more time and alternative supports to confidently and consistently display the behaviors that we model, teach, and reinforce within Tier 1, chapter 4 thoroughly defines the Tier 2 and Tier 3 supports that educators can proactively prepare and provide when a student needs intervention. It provides tools for determining the causes or antecedents of student difficulties and suggests a set of research-based intervention strategies for use with students in Tiers 2 and 3.

The book concludes in chapter 5 with the challenges that practitioners of behavioral RTI have encountered (and that you might experience as well) along with the strategies that we employed to address them.

I and many other educators have experienced the impact that a greater focus on behaviors can have on schools, staff, and, most importantly, student outcomes. I hope the resources in this book will equip your schools to experience similar successes.

Next Steps

The following are next steps in introducing behavioral RTI to your school or team.

- With your staff or teacher teams, have open and honest conversations about the current state of behavioral supports for all students at all tiers.

- Build consensus among your staff or teacher team on the role of schools and educators in developing the habits and attributes associated with behavioral skills.

- Read, share, and synthesize information on the specific behavioral skills that students must develop to be successful students and citizens.

Identifying, Defining, and Making Sense of Behavioral Skills

Psychological factors—often called motivational or non-cognitive factors—can matter even more than cognitive factors for students' academic performance.

— CAROL S. DWECK,
GREGORY M. WALTON,
AND GEOFFREY L. COHEN

If it's predictable, it's preventable. This core phrase is at the heart of RTI. It allows us to identify, anticipate, and prepare for our students' needs, and to proactively respond to these before frustration and disengagement set in. We as educators predict and take measures to prevent student difficulties in academic skills—but how can this *predict-and-prevent* attitude apply to our model of behavioral RTI?

We can predict that a lack of adequate core instruction in the behavioral skills as the introduction describes will compromise student success—both behavioral and academic. We can predict that not all students will possess the mindsets, social skills, perseverance, learning strategies, and academic behaviors that will lead to success in school and life when they arrive in our classrooms. Thus, we can conclude that if we do not identify, prioritize, and teach these critical skills, there will be some students whose success is negatively impacted. We can prevent this negative impact if we establish behavioral skills as a priority along with key academic concepts.

In this chapter, districts, schools, and teams of educators will discover tools to assess the culture of their districts or schools and the readiness of their staff to proactively and positively nurture behavioral skills with and for all students—a necessary precursor to implementing behavioral RTI. They will then consider the first two steps in the behavioral RTI model:

1. **Identify the most critical behavioral skills.**
2. **Define and make sense of these skills.**

Educators will learn to identify those behavioral skills that will most contribute to student success in school, college, career, and life, and define and make sense of what those behavioral skills look and sound like. They will then learn how to prepare both general and content-area-specific behavioral priorities for their classrooms in a manner that emphasizes consistency and prepares them for the next step of teaching behaviors.

So, to begin our journey, let's briefly address school culture.

Creating a Collaborative Culture of Commitment

The first step in designing a system of supports that nurtures the mindsets, social skills, perseverance, learning strategies, and academic behaviors within students—behaviors that are so critical to their success— is for educators to accept responsibility for this critical but challenging task. Parents and communities can positively shape student behaviors, and schools should complement these supports. Schools, however, have the unique opportunity to nurture behavioral skills that educators can apply and practice when engaging in the intellectual tasks in which schools specialize.

The nurturing of behavioral skills is consistent with innovative learning environments in which student voice, choice, and agency are priorities. Ryan Jackson, executive principal of the Mount Pleasant Arts Innovation Zone and practitioner of behavioral RTI, notes that:

> Schools adapting to the Netflix generation mindset, where purpose, passions, and empowerment reign supreme over compliance, standardization, and simple engagement, can be highly successful. These schools are building a sustainable model of behavioral skill success, starting from the ground up with trust and respect as a foundation, and goal setting and commitment as the catalysts. (R. Jackson, personal communication, June 19, 2017)

Creating this sort of staff culture and learning environment starts with a belief in and high expectations for all students' success and a commitment to not letting anything (such as poor attendance, apathy, or deficits in reading skills) get in the way. The central importance of belief and expectations should sound familiar to proponents of PLC at Work (DuFour et al., 2016). They are foundational Big Ideas. A culture of high expectations, of doing whatever it takes, and of recognizing that the only way to ensure that every student learns at high levels is through a commitment to collaborative and collective action has always been at the heart of PLC at Work.

So, how is this nurturing learning environment created? I believe that there exist several foundational principles that educators should address, discuss, and ultimately accept regarding student behavior.

- Behavior is as critical as academics; behavioral skills include the categories of precognitive self-regulation, mindsets, social skills, learning strategies (such as metacognition, cognitive self-regulation, and executive functioning), perseverance, and academic behaviors (such as participation, work completion, attendance, and engagement).

- Students behave and misbehave for a reason, purpose, or function, and educators have a great deal of influence regarding the ways in which students behave.

- Educators must define, model, teach, and nurture the behaviors that they want to see.

- Educators will be most successful nurturing behavioral skills when they align the definitions, steps, and process of *behavioral RTI* to those of *academic RTI*.

- Staff members must assume collective responsibility for nurturing student behaviors.

- Great relationships between educators and educators, educators and students, and students and students lead to better student behavior and greater levels of engagement and learning.

- Great classroom environments with high expectations and clear procedures and routines lead to better student behavior.

- Engaging, rich, and sound pedagogies, strategies, and tasks lead to better student behavior.

- If educators want student behaviors to change, they must be willing to change.

Begin your collective work on building a system of behavioral supports by collaboratively reflecting upon and discussing these foundational ideas, and reference them throughout the process. Do they ring true? Do "yeah, but. . ." and "what if. . ." comments and questions arise? Transparent and courageous dialogue on core principles such as these can help serve as a vision or "North Star" that guides and shapes these critical efforts.

To measure the current realities of your school and the readiness of your staff in creating a nurturing learning environment, consider using the survey in figure 1.1 (page 18) as a preassessment to inform how you will begin your journey. This survey is designed to gauge the current climate and staff attitudes regarding behavior and can be repeated at any time before, during, and after the implementation of the six steps of behavioral RTI.

A colleague was recently appointed principal of a school in which the climate and attitudes, as measured by the survey in figure 1.1, were inhibiting success. Staff were hardworking and capable, but beliefs in all students learning at high levels and a collective commitment to meeting student needs required some attention. This principal courageously and respectfully shared the results with staff and facilitated an open dialogue in which frustrations were expressed. This began a healing process. From this beginning, a grade-level team volunteered to embrace the idea that behavioral skills needed to be taught and time needed to be embedded within the day to do so. The staff members were empowered and supported, and results in the first year, as measured by a reduction in behavioral infractions and increases in attendance, work completion, and reading levels, were dramatic. The momentum and excitement generated from this success inspired other teams to initiate shifts in their practices and a corner had truly been turned; the school now feels different, and student outcomes continue to improve.

Please score with a 1, 2, 3, or 4 each of the following statements:

1—Strongly disagree   **3**—Somewhat agree

2—Somewhat disagree   **4**—Strongly agree

Statement	Score
Staff (teachers, campus supervisors, office staff, cafeteria workers, and so on) know the schoolwide behavioral expectations.	
Staff accept collective responsibility for defining and teaching behavioral expectations.	
Staff consistently model, teach, and nurture behavioral expectations.	
Staff intentionally foster and nurture positive relationships with all students.	
Students know the schoolwide expectations.	
Parents know the schoolwide expectations.	
Follow-through on behavioral infractions is timely.	
Staff clearly communicate follow-through on behavioral infractions.	
Staff view behavioral deficits in the same manner as reading deficits—students lack skills and require supplemental supports.	
After an incident, staff reteach the appropriate behavior skills, ask students to self-reflect, and then guide students toward restitution, in addition to giving consequences.	
Classroom environments promote positive behaviors.	
Lesson designs and topics promote positive behaviors.	
Staff teach the schoolwide expectations to students.	
Staff model schoolwide expectations to students.	
Staff recognize students for displaying desired behaviors more often than they reprimand students for undesired behaviors.	
Staff agree on what type of problem behaviors to refer to the office.	
Staff understand and follow specific steps to initiate intensive supports for vulnerable students.	
The RTI team (principal, administrators, counselors, special education staff, and teachers) uses evidence for making decisions in designing, implementing, and revising behavioral supports.	
The RTI team regularly and efficiently collects evidence of student learning of behavioral expectations.	
Behavior is a focus of schoolwide collaboration discussions and professional development.	

Figure 1.1: Survey of expectations, readiness, strengths, and needs of staff and stakeholders.

*Visit **go.SolutionTree.com/RTI** for a free reproducible version of this figure.*

A commitment to ensuring that all students possess the behavioral skills necessary for readiness in college, a skilled career, and life cannot be fully achieved without providing scaffolded core instruction for every single student, *and* supplemental interventions for students who do not come to school with a mastery of behaviors. We must define, teach, model, and measure mastery of the behavioral skills of all students as part of a core curriculum, both as a distinct and critical part of Tier 1 and integrated into the academic instruction that has far too long represented the totality of a student's school experience. Within the remainder of this chapter, we will describe the process for identifying and defining the behaviors that all students must develop, and give examples of behavioral priorities that schools may consider.

Identifying and Prioritizing Essential Behavioral Skills

Education should have always been about more than academics. Students may earn acceptance into universities and skilled careers through academic achievement, but college is successfully completed and careers are sustained only through the application of behaviors that are too infrequently prioritized and taught in our schools.

Thus, once you have established in your staff a collective belief that behavioral skills are essential to teach and a commitment to make that happen, you must ask two questions: (1) What are the most essential behavioral outcomes that students must master, in order to give them the best possible social and academic outcomes? and (2) What does your team collaboratively agree it will look and sound like when students master these most essential outcomes? These questions are simple to answer in the academic realm, but have not been considered frequently or systematically enough in the context of behavior. We cannot teach behavioral skills without first clearly identifying, prioritizing, and defining those skills that students must possess.

When it comes to academic content, educators are making a renewed commitment to defining a viable curriculum within a grade level or course that all students will master (Larson & Kanold, 2016; Udelhofen, 2014). Next-generation standards and commitments to deeper learning in states and provinces are, in many ways, providing the motivation and opportunity for these endeavors. Depth is increasingly favored over breadth; quality over quantity; mastery over coverage. Educators are prioritizing the concepts and skills that all students must master, ensuring the most critical learning that students must possess receives adequate time and attention. Teams are also more clearly defining what mastery of prioritized content and skills looks like and sounds like. The work of teachers in my district related to these tasks—in kindergarten through twelfth grade, in mathematics, English language arts, science, and history–social science—is innovative and impactful; both teaching and learning are improving. When articulated horizontally and vertically, this collaboration allows for collective professional preparation and ensures that all students are optimally prepared for the next grade level or course.

These processes are not new. From *Understanding by Design* (Wiggins, McTighe, Kiernan, & Frost, 1998) to curriculum mapping (Jacobs, 2004) to *Rigorous Curriculum Design* (Ainsworth, 2010), schools have long recognized that a guaranteed, viable curriculum (Scherer, 2001) is one of the most critical factors contributing to high levels of student learning. In light of next-generation standards, the collaborative staff processes of scoping and sequencing prioritized learning outcomes are more important than ever.

We must apply this very same thinking, and complete this very same work, for the behaviors that we want all students to exhibit. Jim Wright, an RTI trainer and consultant to schools and educational organizations, notes that the "communal initial step of defining community behavior norms actually brings educators into alignment about the conduct they want to foster in their classrooms" (J. Wright, personal communication, May 23, 2017). We must identify, prioritize, describe and define, and scope and sequence these behaviors in our teams and with all staff across the school. In fact, defining and teaching behaviors will require even more consistency and collaboration than defining and teaching academic expectations. Here's why: while collaboration within the third-grade team or high school mathematics department is vital when defining academic priorities for that team, behavioral skills will be expected and practiced within all classrooms on campus. Consistent expectations for appropriate behavioral skills are absolutely critical, no matter a student's grade, no matter the staff member with whom a student is working, and no matter the environment within the school (Buffum, Mattos, & Weber, 2009, 2010, 2012).

So, how do teachers identify these key behaviors? As a first step, form a representative team from across grade levels and departments to identify your school's behavioral priorities using the template in figure 1.2. The prioritization, defining, and teaching of behavioral skills must be consistent across the school; students and staff will be frustrated, confused, and less-than-ideally successful if this is not the case. While all staff must ultimately have a voice in the behavioral skills that are identified, this representative team can guide the process, communicating to and gathering feedback from the colleagues with whom they work.

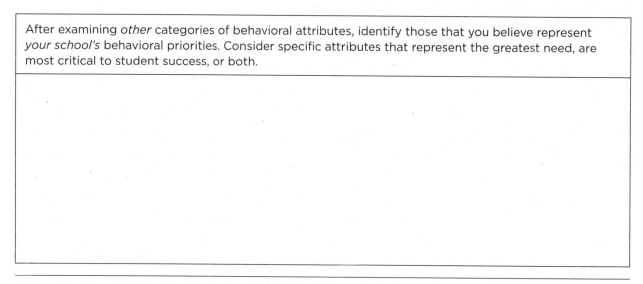

After examining *other* categories of behavioral attributes, identify those that you believe represent *your school's* behavioral priorities. Consider specific attributes that represent the greatest need, are most critical to student success, or both.

Figure 1.2: Template to identify behavioral priorities.

*Visit **go.SolutionTree.com/RTI** for a free reproducible version of this figure.*

To help you identify behavioral priorities, table 1.1 compiles an extensive list of behavioral skills and attributes based on our definition in the introduction, popular educational frameworks, research studies, and models from schools that have successfully implemented RTI. You can use any of these, a combination, or make up your own priorities based on your school's individual needs.

TABLE 1.1: BEHAVIORAL SKILLS AND ATTRIBUTES

Social Behaviors (and Their Opposites): Label and define the behaviors you want to see, not the misbehaviors that you do not want to see.
Social behaviors include: • Cooperation (Disruption)—Interacting positively within learning environment and with others   • Social respect (Defiance)—Complying with expectations   • Physical respect (Aggression)—Demonstrating care and concern for physical being and space of others   • Verbal respect (Inappropriate language)—Using kind, positive, and supportive words   • Attention (Inattention)—Ability to focus   • Self-control (Impulsivity)—Ability to control oneself physically and verbally   • Attendance (Absences)—Physical, cognitive, and emotional presence at school   • Honesty (Lying, cheating, or stealing)—Truthfulness in relationships and learning   • Empathy (Harassment or bullying)—Consideration of others' situations
Academic Behaviors (and Their Opposites): Label and define the behaviors you want to see, not the misbehaviors that you do not want to see.
Academic behaviors include: • Metacognitive practices (Unreflective learning)—Knowledge and beliefs about thinking   • Growth mindset and positive self-concept (Fixed mindset and negative self-talk)—Viewing learning as continuous and intelligence as malleable   • Self-monitoring and internal locus of control (External loci of control)—Ability to plan, prepare, and proceed   • Engagement and motivation (Apathy)—Ability to maintain interest and drive   • Strategy creation and use (Passive learning)—Techniques for construction, organization, and memorization of knowledge   • Volition and perseverance (Learned helplessness)—Efforts students need to maintain their motivation   • Resilience (Emotional fragility)—Techniques for regulating response to situations
Twenty-First Century Skills
These skills mean students know how to: • Access and evaluate information   • Manage projects, goals, and time   • Adapt to change   • Problem solve   • Apply technology   • Produce results   • Be flexible   • Reason effectively   • Be responsible to others   • Self-direct learning   • Collaborate with others in diverse teams   • Think creatively   • Communicate clearly   • Think critically   • Create media products   • Think systematically   • Guide and lead others   • Use and manage information   • Innovate   • Work independently

continued →

College- and Career-Readiness Skills	
• Manage effort and time	• Seek help and self-advocate
• Monitor progress and confirm precision of work	• Self-monitor and self-motivate
• Organize and construct products in various forms	• Set goals
• Persist	• Understand academic expectations for college admission
• Practice self-awareness	• Understand financial aid options and procedures
• Read strategically	• Value knowledge
• Reflect on reasons of success or failure	

Self-Regulation

• Plan, including—	• Reflect, including—
• Goal setting	• Self-advocating
• Strategic thinking	• Self-evaluation
• Manage their time	• Self-assessment
• Monitor—	
• Self-motivation	
• Delaying gratification	
• Attention control	

Executive Functioning

Executive functioning means:

- Setting goals and establishing a due date
- Planning, prioritizing, and sequencing the steps or tasks needed to reach the goal
- Identifying necessary information, materials, or both
- Obtaining and organizing the information, materials needed to complete the goal, or both
- Beginning the task
- Persevering through distractions and delaying gratification
- Establishing a reasonable work rate so that the goal is met by the due date
- Shifting from one task to another smoothly
- Responding to, and incorporating, feedback
- Assessing performance and progress toward the goal
- Controlling emotional responses to difficult situations
- Seeing tasks through to completion

Social-Emotional Learning (SEL) Competencies From CASEL

CASEL lists social-emotional learning competencies as:

- Self-awareness—The ability, within oneself, to recognize how emotions influence behavior; assess strengths and limitations with healthy self-efficacy, optimism, and a growth mindset; and identify emotions
- Self-management—The ability, within oneself, to regulate emotions, thoughts, and behaviors; manage stress; control impulses; be motivated; set goals; and organize
- Social awareness—The ability to empathize with and respect others; understand norms for behavior; and recognize family, school, and community resources and supports
- Relationship management—The ability to establish and maintain healthy and rewarding relationships; communicate clearly; listen well; cooperate with others; resist inappropriate social pressure; negotiate conflict constructively; and seek and offer help
- Responsible decision making—The ability to make choices about behaviors based on ethics, safety, and social norms; evaluate consequences of actions; respect the well-being of oneself and others; identify problems; analyze situations; solve problems; and reflect on and learn from experiences

Learning and Life Strategies	
Conscientiousness	• Reasoning • Empathy • Attention • Awareness of social situations
Optimism	• Belief in oneself • Self-monitoring and self-motivating • Growth mindset and positive self-concept
Metacognition	• Problem solving • Thinking creatively and critically • Analyzing and evaluating findings and viewpoints
Motivation and volition	• Managing projects, goals, and time • Thinking systematically • Employing memorization techniques, study skills, technology skills, and problem-solving strategies • Monitoring progress and confirming the precision of work • Setting short-term and long-term goals • Creating and using strategies
Perseverance	• Practicing self-directed learning • Working independently • Managing effort, time, and materials
Relationships	• Collaborating responsibly with others in diverse teams • Communicating clearly and persuasively • Guiding and leading others • Managing relationships • Being aware of emotions • Making responsible decisions
Resilience	• Adaptability to change • Flexibility • Persistence
Self-advocacy	• Focusing on an interest or career pathway or major • Being self-aware • Reflecting on reasons of success or failure and seeking help • Communicating in written, verbal, and social ways

continued ➡

Examples of School or Agency's Lists of Behavioral Skills	
Knowledge is Power Program (KIPP): • Grit • Self-control • Zest • Social intelligence • Gratitude • Optimism • Curiosity **Character Counts!:** • Trustworthiness • Respect • Responsibility • Fairness • Caring • Citizenship **Scholarly Attributes:** • Respect yourself and others • Make good decisions • Solve your own problems	**Three *Rs*:** • **R**espect • **R**esponsibility • **R**eadiness **Three *Ss*:** • **S**trategy • **S**elf-efficacy • **S**elf-starting **REAL:** • **R**espect • **E**ffort • **A**ttitude • **L**eadership **Three *Ms*:** • **M**otivation • **M**etacognition • **M**onitoring **MOP:** • **M**otivation • **O**rganization • **P**erseverance **PRIDE:** • **P**ositive • **R**esponsible • **I**ntegrity • **D**ependable • **E**ngage

*Visit **go.SolutionTree.com/RTI** for a free reproducible version of this table.*

Next, consider your behavioral priorities in greater detail in the context of our behavioral RTI framework. You will find a simple template in figure 1.3 (page 26) for categorizing behavioral priorities into the five areas Farrington et al.'s (2012) framework defines. Within each of the five areas, we suggest identifying three key behaviors to focus on. While PBIS-oriented behavioral models typically include three to four skills, and Knowledge is Power Program (KIPP) schools very successfully emphasize seven, our behavioral RTI template suggests fifteen behavioral skills to prioritize (see figure 1.3, page 26, and, as examples, the Key Behavioral Skills row in figure 1.4, page 27). KIPP schools are charter schools whose emphasis on developing skills within students that research indicates are most necessary for success—skills described in this book—was profiled in *How Children Succeed* (Tough, 2012). Though this may seem like a large number, I urge educators to consider that there are forty-two English language arts standards in each grade within the Common Core State Standards (ten reading literature, ten reading informational text, ten writing, six language, and six listening and speaking, plus four foundational skill standards in grades K–5)—and that's before we further define the sub-standards and learning targets within each standard (National Governors Association Center for Best Practices & Council of Chief State School Officers, 2010). If behavior is as critical as academics for success in school, college, career, and life, then we should be open to prioritizing a few more critical behavioral skills than we are used to. Of course, each school and school system should decide what is most necessary for its students—indeed, you may choose more than three per factor. The fifteen skills that I suggest simply provide more detail and definition to the categories Farrington and her colleagues (2012) describe.

Consider this important note: I have not included precognitive self-regulation as a separate column within the behavioral skills template. While I acknowledge the critical importance and presence of these foundations, schools and educators will not and cannot "teach" basic health, nutrition, and sleep into existence in the same way that we can and must nurture the skills in table 1.1 (page 21). Instead, we can and must work with families, social agencies, and governmental groups by proactively and passionately striving to determine family needs and reimagining schools so that they represent hubs of community to ensure that the students' physiological and safety needs are met. Additionally, we will discuss ways to mitigate the impact of needs in the area of precognitive self-regulation in chapter 4, page 120. We can positively impact students' precognitive self-regulatory skills through emphasizing their practice both within and outside schools and by supporting students' emotional coping skills, which we believe are subsumed within the five skill areas in figure 1.3 (page 26).

To *define* the behaviors that staff have prioritized, teams should *describe* what the displayed behavioral skills will look like and sound like. To illustrate how to fill out the template, figure 1.4 (page 27) contains a suggestion for behavioral skills that schools may prioritize. It also provides examples of how to describe each of these behaviors. The examples of behavioral priorities in figure 1.4 are suggestions only; we strongly recommend that staff analyze their students' specific needs and select the essential behaviors that they feel will best prepare students in their particular neighborhoods and districts for the next year of schooling and for life. The following recommended categories of behaviors—categories that are used and further described throughout the book—are simply the categories that Farrington and colleagues' (2012) review of the research indicates are most critical for success. They include needs that educators probably recognize in their students and about which educators have been reading, including mindsets, grit or perseverance, and social-emotional learning.

Teacher or staff teams can identify and describe these behaviors within their teams or in collaboration with students. One principal who utilizes the collaborative process when prioritizing and defining behavioral skills is Jon Swett, principal of Shaw Middle School, Washington, and noted pioneer of behavioral RTI. He says:

> At Shaw, we establish schoolwide and classroom agreements with our students rather [than] dictate rules. This opens the door for us to ask students to tell us how they want us to hold them accountable to the social and academic goals we set. (J. Swett, personal communication, June 9, 2017)

Principal Swett's point is important: students and parents, in addition to teaching and support staff, should be involved in the process of determining and defining these behavioral skills, attitudes, attributes, and habits. We want and need the support and involvement of parents and students' voices about skills they need for success in school, college, career, and life. Additionally, this will lead to a greater student understanding of why these non-academic skills are being emphasized.

Behavioral Factors	Academic mindsets	Social skills	Academic perseverance	Learning strategies	Academic behaviors
Key Behavioral Skills	Students: • • • • • • • • • •	Students: • • • • • • • • • •	Students: • • • • • • • • • •	Students: • • • • • • • • • •	Students: • • • • • • • • • •
Descriptions	Students: • • • • • • • • • •	Students: • • • • • • • • • •	Students: • • • • • • • • • •	Students: • • • • • • • • • •	Students: • • • • • • • • • •

Figure 1.3: Template for identifying and describing key behavioral skills.

Visit go.SolutionTree.com/RTI for a free reproducible version of this figure.

Behavioral Factors	Academic mindsets	Social skills	Academic perseverance	Learning strategies	Academic behaviors
Key Behavioral Skills	Students: • Engage • Believe • Belong	Students: • Respect • Cooperate • Empathize	Students: • Persevere • Adapt • Advocate	Students: • Regulate • Reflect • Monitor	Students: • Attend • Complete • Participate
Descriptions	Students: • View learning as continuous and intelligence as malleable • Express optimism • Believe in oneself • Maintain interest and drive • Seek relevance and purpose in learning • Seek ways to belong • Communicate clearly and persuasively • Practice self-awareness	Students: • Interact positively within learning environments and with adults and classmates • Behave and collaborate responsibly • Comply with expectations • Manage relationships • Demonstrate care and concern for the physical being and space of others • Use kind, positive, and supportive words • Practice truthfulness in relationships and learning • Display consideration of others' situations and emotions • Regulate responses to social situations	Students: • Reflect on reasons for success or failure • Seek assistance • Adapt to changes • Respond flexibly to temporary obstacles • Maintain effort • Monitor progress toward goals, projects, effort, and time • Self-direct learning • Work independently • Exercise self-control • Assertively engage in learning • Practice productive work habits • Manage time	Students: • Think metacognitively • Set short-term and long-term goals • Problem solve • Think creatively and critically • Plan, prepare, and proceed • Analyze and evaluate findings and viewpoints • Monitor progress and confirm the precision of work • Employ techniques for constructing, organizing, and remembering • Utilize memorization techniques	Students: • Are present—physically, cognitively, and emotionally • Organize resources • Focus, even when presented with distractors • Complete work • Participate in school and class • Employ study skills

Figure 1.4: Examples of behavioral priorities.

What you choose to name your behavioral priorities isn't as important, and the specific behavioral priorities that teams select are not as important, as the selection of a viable quantity of behavioral priorities that you can consistently define, teach, and reinforce. Just as with academic skills, depth is more important than breadth. Schools may choose to begin by prioritizing behavioral skills with what they see as the greatest student need. As an example of prioritizing behavioral skills, behavioral RTI consultant Jim Wright believes that:

> A prime inhibitor of student success is learned helplessness, the self-reinforcing syndrome in which the student assumes that poor school performance is tied to their own lack of ability rather than a need to apply more effort. So . . . the behavioral skill most critical to success is self-efficacy, the confidence within the student that he or she can meet any academic task through the application of effort and self-regulation skills. (J. Wright, personal communication, May 23, 2017)

Thus, prioritizing self-efficacy-related attributes such as engaging, believing, belonging, persevering, adapting, and advocating (from figure 1.4, page 27) may be a first step for schools with which Wright works.

Consistency is key. When different expectations, interpretations, and applications of the behaviors that they expect students to display exist between classrooms, educators will be frustrated and students will be unsuccessful. Wright notes:

> [The] variability of behavioral norms across classrooms creates confusion—and is a prime driver of student misbehavior . . . minimizing this discrepancy by getting teachers to agree up front on what shared set of "goal" student behaviors they will preteach substantially reduces the "friction" in interactions between students and teachers (and among students as well). (J. Wright, personal communication, May 23, 2017)

In addition to consistency, high expectations are key to success. When educators establish high expectations for student success in conjunction with student participation, students recognize that their teachers and principal believe that they can achieve these behavioral skills at high levels, and they rise to the occasion.

But what does achievement at high levels look like? The next important step in behavioral RTI is to define your chosen behavioral skills. This will be discussed in the following section.

Defining Key Behavioral Skills

Once you identify your key behavioral priorities, a representative team of staff, students, stakeholders, or all of these, should fully and purposefully engage in defining what the behavioral priorities look like and sound like. Identifying behavioral priorities is not enough. We as educators must also clearly and consistently define these priorities in ways that allow us to observe and measure success. At Shaw Middle School, Principal Jon Swett and staff focus on the same behavioral skills (or noncognitive factors) that KIPP adopts—grit, self-control, zest, social intelligence, gratitude, optimism, and curiosity. Staff use the school's character report card throughout the school year as a way for students to monitor and reflect on their strengths and weaknesses. Swett explains, "They set social goals and become aware of themselves as learners. This is how our students get good grades—through research-based best practices" (personal communication, June 9, 2017). Setting goals for what success looks like allows the students to optimize their learning and empowers them by giving them *agency*, or the opportunity to influence their own life and learning path.

Defining academic concepts, content, and skills is important—and challenging! So, give this process an adequate amount of time to complete. Principal Derek McCoy of West Rowan Middle School, North Carolina, notes that:

> We need to define the expectations clearly. At West Rowan Middle, we have developed our core values that outline what our school is looking for in learners—compassion, communication, collaboration, integrity, and purpose. We drill down all of those into specific things we want to see. We don't make it about "Don't do this, don't do that"; it is about what we want to see and the lesson or activities in which students participate. This is more celebration and showcase rather than punitive measures. (D. McCoy, personal communication, June 6, 2017)

Include many voices and opinions—staff, students, parents, community—and provide these stakeholders with the information on critical skills (such as the information provided in the introduction) that may shape their inputs. These voices may be included through a series of multi-stakeholder meetings. We recommend the use of interest-based decision-making processes. Provide time for review, reflection, and revision. But never lose sight of why you engage in this critical work: behaviors are as critical to success in school, college, career, and life as academics, and we have not yet sufficiently addressed these skills in schools.

To ensure that clarity exists on what it will look and sound like when students display the behavioral skills, teams should complete figure 1.5.

Key behavioral skills or priority: Describe in specific detail, using observable and measurable characteristics, what the behavioral priority looks like and sounds like.		
	What does it look like?	**What does it sound like?**
During Whole-Group Instruction		
During Small-Group Instruction		
Within the Classroom		
Outside the Classroom		

Figure 1.5: Template to prioritize what behavioral skills should look and sound like.

*Visit **go.SolutionTree.com/RTI** for a free reproducible version of this figure.*

Figure 1.6 is an example for the key behavioral skills of *engage*, *believe*, and *belong*. We chose this example because many educators identify a lack of a growth mindset (or a lack of motivation, or a sense of apathy) as one of the most significant behavioral concerns that exist for students within their classrooms.

Key behavioral skills or priority: Engage, believe, and belong		
Describe in specific detail, using observable and measurable characteristics, what the priority looks like and sounds like.		
	What does it look like?	**What does it sound like?**
During Whole-Group Instruction	Students are displaying positive nonverbals (smiling, nodding, responding, and so on).	Students are asking questions that focus on the learning outcomes and their intrinsic interests.
During Small-Group Instruction	Students are actively working, exploring inside of their personalized learning path.	Students are inquiring, discussing, and conjecturing.
Within the Classroom	Students are interacting in a collaborative nature. Students are moving about with energy and excitement.	Students are presenting ideas, affirming each other, and providing feedback.
Outside the Classroom	Students are reflecting through writing, blogging, or both.	Students are debating and initiating conversations about learning.

Figure 1.6: Example for what *engage*, *believe*, and *belong* look and sound like.

Schoolwide teams should scope and sequence prioritized *academic* concepts and skills throughout the school year in a manner that favors depth over breadth, mastery over coverage, and quality over quantity—we must plan a guaranteed and viable curriculum (Scherer, 2001). The same applies to *behavioral* skills. For example, a high school team might determine that all staff and students will focus on engaging, believing, and belonging (key elements of academic mindsets) in the month of October, with the math department taking the lead on developing minilessons for the entire staff. The team might then determine that all staff and students will focus on respect, cooperation, and empathy (key social skills) in the month of November, with the science department taking the lead on developing minilessons for the entire staff. In support and in collaboration with the incredible team at Anderson County High School in Lawrenceburg, Kentucky, I developed the following eight units of instruction in figure 1.7, that correspond to eight academic units of instruction (two per quarter). While this scope and sequence recommends relative areas of focus, the staff model, nurture, embed, and reinforce all behavioral skills. Scopes and sequences will likely vary based on grade level, student needs, and the number of years a school has been engaged in this important work.

Anderson County High School dedicates two days a week of their advisory period to the teaching and learning of these behavioral skills, with the schoolwide minilessons created by different teams of teachers. And importantly, the skills are emphasized and reinforced throughout the rest of the day and week.

All Anderson County schools, and Anderson County High School in particular, recognize that we must devote the same energies and intelligence to prioritizing and defining behavioral skills as we have appropriately devoted to academic skills. Behaviors are not just prerequisites to learning academic priorities; behavioral skills are as critical to learn as academic skills.

Unit 1	Unit 2	Unit 3	Unit 4
Frontload all behavioral priorities during the first four to six weeks of the year, while establishing productive routines, procedures, expectations, and relationships that lead to positive school and classroom contexts.	Focus more on *engage, believe,* and *belong.*	Focus more on *respect, cooperate,* and *empathize.*	Focus more on *attend, complete,* and *participate.*
Unit 5	**Unit 6**	**Unit 7**	**Unit 8**
Focus more on *persevere, adapt,* and *advocate.*	Focus more on *regulate, reflect,* and *monitor.*	Review and revisit skills for which there is evidence of relative need.	Prepare students for productive summers or inter-sessions and for a productive beginning of the next school year.

Figure 1.7: Scope and sequence of eight units of instruction.

And let's not miss an opportunity for addressing two critical topics with an integrated approach. Many schools are defining and teaching digital citizenship as part of blended, digitally rich shifts in teaching and learning and as part of appropriate-use and responsible-use policies. The International Society for Technology in Education (ISTE) identifies nine elements of digital citizenship around topics such as equality, etiquette, honesty, communication, self-monitoring, safety, and health (Ribble, 2014). Consider combining *Behavior: The Forgotten Curriculum; An RTI Approach for Nurturing Essential Life Skills* efforts with digital citizenship policies, and provide students with opportunities to practice and apply the behavioral skills that they are learning. Strive to align the habits and attributes that we are nurturing within students, whether online or in person.

Identifying and Defining Behaviors in Content-Specific Areas

Teachers will experience the greatest success in ensuring that students develop positive and productive behavioral skills when a high degree of consistency exists among educators' understanding of behavioral skills and implementation of behavioral instruction and reinforcement (Gregory et al., 2010; Skiba & Peterson, 2000). However, while behavioral skills are largely common across all contexts, there is also value in defining what your school's chosen fifteen skills look like and sound like within specific content areas.

The specific questions, strategies, and tasks an English teacher employs in nurturing metacognition among students may be slightly different than a teacher of mathematics. Each domain and even problem type may require different strategies to tackle difficult tasks. What should a student who can't seem to get started writing a paper do to persevere? What about the student stuck on a mathematics word problem or struggling through a reading passage? When would it be helpful to make a list, draw a picture, or even take a break? What can the student do to learn from prior attempts and the attempts of others when it comes to writing, comprehending, or calculating?

Figure 1.8 provides descriptions for the same set of skills contained in figure 1.4 (page 27), but in this case, the descriptions are specifically tailored to a mathematics course. You can adapt behavioral skill descriptions for any course, grade level, or even cocurricular activity.

Schoolwide descriptions of what essential behaviors look like and sound like are a must. Content-specific or departmental-specific descriptions can help students clearly understand expectations in context and help teachers embrace and make sense of these behaviors in their individual classrooms.

Conclusion

A lack of adequate core instruction in behavioral skills will compromise student success—in school, college, career, and life. We can predict that not all students will enter our classrooms possessing the mindsets, social skills, perseverance, learning strategies, and academic behaviors to optimally succeed in schools. For our most vulnerable students, a proactive set of core supports is life-saving. For all students, these skills will add so much value to their educational experience and prepare them even more comprehensively for life.

Chapter 1 provided educators with tools to assess the culture of their school and the readiness of their staff to proactively and positively nurture behavioral skills with and for all students. It then offered resources for helping educators identify and clearly define those behavioral skills they see as key to success. However, defining behavioral content is not enough. We must model, teach, and nurture the exhibition of behaviors that will lead to successful school, career, and life experiences. These important topics will be the focus of the next chapter.

Next Steps

The following are next steps in identifying and defining key behavioral skills for students in your school or district.

- Bring together a group of stakeholders to frame the needs and opportunities around nurturing students' behavioral skills. Consider surveying students and parents with the survey in figure 1.1 (page 18) to complement data from the survey of staff members.

- Ask staff, parents, and students about the behaviors that are of biggest concern and the behaviors they believe are most important to success. Agree on a set of behavioral skills and define and communicate what mastery of these skills looks like.

- Involve students in defining what the prioritized behavioral skills will look and sound like. Empower students to communicate expectations to their classmates.

Behavioral Factors	Academic mindsets	Social skills	Academic perseverance	Learning strategies	Academic behaviors
Key Behavioral Skills	Students: • Engage • Believe • Belong	Students: • Respect • Cooperate • Empathize	Students: • Persevere • Adapt • Advocate	Students: • Regulate • Reflect • Monitor	Students: • Attend • Complete • Participate
Descriptions	Students: • View mistakes as opportunities • Recomplete incorrect or less-than-complete solutions • Engage fully with problems for which there is more than one approach and for which there is more than one correct solution • Regularly try more than one approach, even when initially successful • Resist immediately asking for assistance and accept temporary struggle • Find and share real-world applications of mathematics • Devote authentic time to setting a purpose and making connections • Encourage the identification of patterns • Regularly complete mathematics problems, logic puzzles, and mental mathematics activities	Students: • Interact positively within learning environments and with adults and classmates • Behave and collaborate responsibly • Comply with expectations • Manage relationships • Demonstrate care and concern for the physical being and space of others • Use kind, positive, and supportive words • Practice truthfulness in relationships and learning • Display consideration of others' situations and emotions • Regulate responses to social situations	Students: • Utilize tech tools to record or write out reactions to problems when encountering them initially • Problem solve via a *talk aloud* or *think aloud*, specifically honing in on what is known, not known, and strategies that have been helpful in the past (drawing, sketching, collaborating, and so on) • Accept that complex problems will take time, and parallel this concept to the fact that many exciting and puzzling life problems take time to uncover	Students: • Reflect on how a problem was solved, what it was about, or where and why a difficulty occurred in the process of problem solving • Test approaches and verify accuracies, creating and using plans of action • Create or use conceptually sound mnemonics • Analyze errors regularly, looking for patterns • Create personalized checklists to use when completing problems and reviewing the accuracy of solutions • Adapt existing and initial procedures (while retaining the conceptual accuracy of the heuristic) to personal habits and preferences • Prepare and normalize the use of sufficient space and multiple attempts to solve problems • Reflect via self-assessment tools to assess proximity toward mastery	Students: • Connect mathematics problems to existing knowledge • Strive for learning progress and mastery of the learning target • Participate fully in problem solving within the classroom • Create a list of problems (add to your list throughout the year) and propose multiple approaches and ways to solve the problem • Evaluate other's strategies or approaches and choose the best or most appropriate strategy for the scenario

Figure 1.8: Behavior skills examined through the subject of mathematics.

Modeling, Teaching, and Nurturing Behavioral Skills

When noncognitive factors are in place, students will look—and be—motivated. In fact, these noncognitive factors constitute what psychological researchers call motivation, and fostering these mindsets and self-regulation strategies is what psychological researchers typically mean by motivating students.

— CAROL S. DWECK,
GREGORY M. WALTON, AND
GEOFFREY L. COHEN

Consider Billy's story: Billy is a student who cannot successfully divide three-digit numbers by two-digit numbers. Most students in Billy's class come into the grade knowing how to divide multidigit numbers, even though this standard is an expectation at Billy's grade level. Billy is not behind in relation to grade-level standards but he does appear behind in relation to his classmates. Billy's teacher notices this struggle, tells Billy that his errors are unacceptable, and informs Billy that he has one more chance to demonstrate his ability to correctly solve a multidigit problem. Otherwise, he will receive a check next to his name and may be sent to the office. Billy is no further in his capacity to solve the problem after this additional chance and continues to struggle. The teacher tells Billy he has run out of opportunities and will now need to receive a punishment as a result of his difficulty dividing multidigit numbers.

We all recognize the absurdity of this situation. You're undoubtedly thinking that Billy needs to be taught strategies to solve this problem and that differentiated approaches and scaffolds may be necessary. You recognize that Billy would benefit from Tier 2 support—more time and alternative strategies to master this essential mathematical skill. You might even predict that Billy's difficulties with division stem from deficits in foundational mathematics skills—difficulties with number sense or difficulties with basic computation—which will require Tier 3 supports.

Yet if the same scenario related to a behavioral challenge, many would note that this scenario is common; others may even feel that it is reasonable. We too often, and inappropriately, view behavioral struggles differently than academic struggles. Behavior and academics are inextricably linked, and teaching, learning, assessing, and implementing differentiated supports of behavioral skills and academic skills deserve equal attention.

We often encounter students with challenges in mastering academic skills for whom behavioral difficulties are a contributing factor. We also encounter students whose misbehaviors are significantly impacted by years of academic frustration and failure. Behavioral and academic skills are not only complementary but can also be dependent on each other. We as educators must commit to defining and making sense of teaching, modeling, and measuring behaviors—by all staff and for all students.

Thus far, we have nurtured a culture of collective commitment in which all staff accept responsibility for helping all students develop all the skills, including behavioral skills, that they need to succeed in school, college, career, and life. Also, we have identified and defined and made sense of a set of behavioral priorities, with all stakeholders, that we commit to consistently and positively nurturing within all students. Now, we need to focus on the third of the six steps of behavioral RTI:

> 3. **Model, teach, and nurture these skills.**

We must plan for how we will model, teach, and nurture prioritized behavioral skills so that these attributes are sufficiently nurtured and so that all students experience success.

This chapter begins with discussing the initial focus on Tier 1 before moving on to the need for universal screening to help educators better prepare and scaffold proactive supports. It will then focus on several methods to successfully teach, model, nurture, practice, and reinforce behavioral skills, aligning the definitions, steps, and processes of academic RTI to behavioral RTI. Next, it discusses the need for positive, nurturing relationships within behavioral RTI. By the end of this chapter, educators will be prepared to design behavioral learning experiences embedded within the teaching and learning of academic concepts and skills as well as minilessons that explicitly address prioritized behaviors. Finally, they will prioritize establishing positive relationships with every single student—no matter what, no matter who, whatever it takes.

Focusing on Tier 1

Hardworking and committed teachers across the world find student behavior frustrating within their classrooms. They acknowledge that, while 95 percent of the class behaves appropriately and compliantly, 5 percent of students demand a lot of attention, and at times, this 5 percent can derail the normal and positive flow of teaching and learning (Ennis, 1996; Way, 2011). Teachers recognize that this 5 percent are highly vulnerable and in need, and that students often have experienced, or are experiencing, trauma in their lives away from school.

We have two related responses to teachers in these situations, responses that we have put into action within our schools. First, we can do better for the 95 percent. Passive compliance is not our goal; rather, students must become authentically engaged in their learning and growth to succeed in school and life (Schlechty, 2002). The 95 percent deserve and will benefit from modeling, teaching, practice, and support on well-defined behavioral priorities that will contribute to their social and functional success. Second, the 5 percent of students who are providing definitive evidence that they desperately need relationally based nurturing of behaviors will not be successful without differentiated core supports for academics and behaviors. Highly vulnerable students will likely need intensive, Tier 3 supports (described in chapter 4, page 119). However, they also deserve and need differentiated Tier 1 supports in behavior. We cannot expect that students will develop the behavioral skills that they must possess unless we take responsibility for providing these comprehensive core supports.

As a result, we present in the behavioral RTI model a renewed focus on Tier 1 behavior and the nurturing of noncognitive skills. To be clear, we are admirers and followers of the tenets of positive behavior interventions and supports (Sugai & Horner, 2002) and other efforts at inculcating a consistent set of expectations across a school. And yet, we repeatedly hear that student misbehaviors, apathy, and disorganization are inhibiting learning. Many existing approaches offer plans for improving student behavior through a classroom-management lens, and evidence exists of their success (Sugai, 2001; Sugai & Horner, 2002). Yet, schools continue to struggle with the student motivation and academic success for all and are seeking other options.

Building on the principles of PLC at Work, RTI, and PBIS, we are attempting to accomplish the following in our behavioral RTI model.

- Employ the same planning procedures, with the same emphases, for the teaching and learning of behavioral skills as we follow for the teaching and learning of academic skills.

- Make explicit the connection between academics and behaviors, and embed the teaching and learning of behavioral skills into the teaching and learning of academic skills.

- Elevate the teaching and learning of behavioral skills to their rightful place alongside academic skills.

- Blend these complementary sets of behavioral skills (for example, self-regulation, executive functioning, social-emotional learning, academic mindsets, and restorative practices) into Tier 1.

We do not need to be behaviorists—specialists in the study of behavior—to follow the behavioral RTI model. We simply need to commit to nurturing skills and relationships and to learning what we need to accomplish these goals. Our work should be in conjunction with parents and communities to complement the care and support they provide when students are not in school.

Teaching behaviors requires a collaborative approach greater even than the need for collaboration when planning for the teaching and learning of academic skills (Buffum et al., 2009, 2010, 2012). While we must engage in both horizontal and vertical articulation for essential academic skills (such as mathematics), behavioral expectations must be the same across all adults, subject areas, and environments in the school. In my school and district experiences, a failure to align behavioral priorities and expectations, instructional practices, assessment measures, and differentiated practices across the breadth of a school severely compromises students' chances at mastering behavioral skills. We must expect students to practice effective self-regulatory strategies, for example, no matter the adult with whom they are learning and working, no matter the subject area, no matter the time of day, and no matter the physical setting.

Teaching behavioral skills within Tier 1 means we must erase the *can't do–won't do* distinction. A student labeled as lacking the will to succeed lacks proficiency in certain behavioral skills, just as a student experiencing difficulties comprehending text lacks proficiency in certain reading skills. His or her lack of proficiency stems from some underlying cause, just as there is an underlying cause of academic difficulties. Our successful approach to meeting all students' behavioral needs starts with a well-defined, explicitly taught, and robust Tier 1—just as it does for academic skills.

We believe that we can, and must, significantly improve our Tier 1 behavioral supports for all students. We can achieve this by:

- Clearly defining the content—the behavioral expectations for students—by all staff, within all environments of the school, which we addressed in the previous chapter (page 15)

- Consistently and explicitly modeling and teaching the behaviors we want to see and hear

- Integrating this instruction into academics

- Gathering evidence about the extent to which all students are meeting behavioral expectations

- Gaining timely evidence regarding students who are not adequately served by Tier 1 supports

We have identified and defined the most critical behavioral skills, which are steps 1 and 2 of the six steps described in the introduction (page 1). This chapter focuses on step 3: modeling, teaching, and nurturing these skills.

A schoolwide behavior plan can often, unfortunately, become focused on compliance or on control. We acknowledge that there are vulnerable students with more immediate behavioral needs for whom we can and must provide immediate and intensive supports, in addition to the core instruction described within this chapter. This will be discussed in chapter 4 (page 93). However, we believe that we can better diagnose the specific behavioral needs of students. We believe that we can better support these students. This superior support starts with proactive screening and support at Tier 1.

Instead of focusing on classroom management, consequences, or students getting what they deserve, so that other students get the message that *this type of misbehavior* is unacceptable, we must prepare *all* students to manage and monitor their behaviors, their learning, and their emotions. Through his work in hundreds of schools, Stuart Shanker (2012), a worldwide leading authority on self-regulation and child development, has demonstrated that all students will benefit from developing strategies to set themselves up for success and to recognize, anticipate, and successfully navigate stressors within multiple environments. For our most vulnerable students, these stressors are simply much more present.

For these vulnerable students, an insufficient catalogue of self-regulatory strategies may be significantly contributing to their difficulties. The unfortunate response of some educators is that there's something wrong with students, that their parents are to blame, that their parents must do more, and that educators cannot help these students until the situation improves. But this attitude is unnecessarily hopeless. Students can translate the positive social and emotional experiences that occur within our classrooms into information they can use to regulate thoughts, emotions, and behaviors (Blair & Diamond, 2008). *We* are the answer we've been waiting for. We can partner with parents and communities to develop students' behavioral skills. And we can equip ourselves with tools to nurture the requisite skills within students.

Before we begin teaching and modeling behavioral skills, there are certain skills that we as educators must first possess. We will discuss these in the following section.

Preparing Educators to Model and Teach Behavioral Skills

If we as educators would like to see changes in student behaviors, and if we commit to doing whatever it takes to serve all students and ensure that all students achieve at high levels, then we must also prepare ourselves. While you have already established a culture of collective commitment to the need for a curriculum of behavioral supports in your school (see chapter 1, page 15), it is also important to establish a shared vision of how to integrate these supports and to establish a safe, positive environment that engages your students. It is also crucial to develop, within each individual teacher, the attributes necessary to nurture such practices in others.

Behavioral skill planning, instruction, and assessment will continue to be an afterthought if not integrated into all aspects of the teaching and learning process with consistency. This shift begins with a commitment to integration. The integration of behavior and academics will only be effective if there is a true belief that the two are complementary and interdependent. We should apply the same vocabulary, thinking, and processes to planning and implementing Tier 1 behavioral instruction as we apply to planning and implementing Tier 1 academic instruction.

There are some who will not believe that it is their job to teach behavioral skills; others who do not believe that they have the time; and still others who do not believe they possess the skills. If not us, then who? We will achieve when we make a commitment to nurturing behavioral skills; when we make the time to define, model, and teach these skills in our classroom; and when we consider academic and behavioral skills as two sides of the same coin. The coin, in this case, is readiness for college, career, and life. Integration applies to how we prepare and implement. In the last chapter (page 15), we applied curriculum mapping processes to behavioral skills, just as so often we have applied them to academics. In this chapter, we will apply what we know about best practices in the teaching of academic skills to the teaching of behavioral skills.

High-quality instruction in both academics and behaviors requires a school culture and classroom community where every student feels safe and affirmed and is fully engaged. Knowing students is the key to growing students; student growth in both academics and behaviors requires that staff commit to improvements in our relational skills with students and our pedagogical skills in facilitating the teaching and learning process. This will be discussed in the section Nurturing Skills Through Relationships later in this chapter (page 52).

Understanding the complexities of behavior requires that we understand the complexities of communication. Communication is a vital skill, and while students often have a difficult time with understanding what they are communicating and the implications of what has been perceived, adults also struggle with communication. We should reflect on our communication and ensure that none of our words leave students feeling angry, misunderstood, judged, or devalued. As Jim Wright notes, "Helping educators to adopt positive communication as a routine, consistent 'habit' should be the goal of every school" (personal communication, May 23, 2017). Richard Curwin and Allen Mendler's (1999) work provides guidance in the area of communication. In my own experience, my staffs collectively created and maintained a list of "things we should never say to students" and "things we should say to students" in an honest effort to communicate positively with students and give honest recognition that we haven't always succeeded.

Finally, we must prepare to teach behavioral skills by developing our own precognitive skills. Precognitive self-regulatory skills involve:

- Learning how to read, reframe, and redefine student misbehaviors
- Assuming that every student has the capacity to change
- Teaching, modeling, and nurturing appropriate behaviors as a preventative endeavor
- Helping students recognize stressors
- Guiding students to master the steps involved in self-awareness
- Ameliorating causes of high stress within schools, in neighborhoods and homes, and in collaboration with community partners
- Reframing misbehaviors as stress behaviors

There is no magic formula or shortcut to developing these skills. These skills will only be improved through courageous and vulnerable self-reflection, professional learning, and collaborative practices with our colleagues as we seek to continuously improve.

Certain districts or areas, depending on the student population, may require teachers to develop specialized skills, such as an understanding of trauma. This was the case at Shaw Middle School, where, according to Principal Jon Swett:

> A big area of initial growth was understanding trauma. The book *Help for Billy* and the guidance provided by Kent Hoffman helped us develop and define what it looks like and sounds like to become "strong, kind, and committed" with our students and to not take student behaviors personally. (J. Swett, personal communication, June 19, 2017)

Empathy is a critical skill for students to develop; we can be the model. But first, we have to be prepared.

Continuing the theme of preparation, the next step in implementing behavioral skill teaching is to prepare proactive supports for students in need. We can achieve this with universal screening.

Screening Students

We have already established the behavioral skills that will help ensure students succeed in school, college, career, and life (see chapter 1, page 15). The next step is to identify which students—based on evidence, data, and observations—are likely to require immediate and relatively intensive supports from the very beginning of the year to achieve success. We can predict that some students will have behavioral skill needs—needs that we can and should determine early within school years and school careers. We can prevent frustrations and failures by screening for these needs and proactively preparing positive supports.

Universal screening is a popular RTI term. What does it mean? First of all, we do not screen to label or confirm the reasons that a student is succeeding or having difficulties. We screen so that we actively anticipate students in need and proactively prepare positive supports. This is a foundational principle of RTI.

Screening filters those students who are at risk of failure unless they receive immediate, intensive supports. Remember, if it's predictable, it's preventable. One efficient and practical way in which to screen students is to reflect on those students for whom mastery of the prioritized and defined behavioral skills proves to be quite difficult. We can predict who these students are—they scored in the lowest performance band on the state (or province) test; they scored in the sixth percentile on a norm-referenced test; they were suspended for twelve days last year. At the end of each academic year, teachers should screen all students in this manner to identify any individuals who, despite a strong core instructional program (Tier 1), are still in danger of failure. To ensure that students do not fall further and further behind, students must have access to immediate help (Buffum et al., 2009, 2010, 2012; Hierck, Coleman, & Weber, 2011). Those determined to be at risk for experiencing significant difficulties receive targeted, evidence-based interventions as soon as is practical.

I will now discuss two tools for screening students: the combined student risk screening scale and student internalizing behavior screening scale, and transition guides.

Student Risk Screening Scale and Student Internalizing Behavior Screening Scale

Two tools that schools may use when screening all students in the area of behavioral skills are the *student risk screening scale* (SRSS; Drummond, 1994) and the *student internalizing behavior screening scale* (SIBSS; Cook et al., 2011). The SRSS and SIBSS are brief, no-cost, research-based screeners that educators can use to identify students with externalizing and internalizing behavioral challenges. (For research on the use and efficacy of these screeners, please see Lane, Bruhn, Eisner, & Kalberg, 2010; Lane, Kalberg, Lambert, Crnobori, & Bruhn, 2010; Lane, Kalberg, Parks, & Carter, 2008; Lane et al., 2009; Lane et al., 2011; Lane, Parks, Kalberg, & Carter, 2007; Menzies & Lane, 2012; Oakes et al., 2010). I have combined these measures into one overarching, universal template in figure 2.1 (page 42).

Teacher name:

Please rate both the SRSS and SIBSS separately in the following boxes. Use the following scale.

- 0—Never
- 1—Occasionally
- 2—Sometimes
- 3—Frequently

Totals:

- 0 to 3 indicates low risk.
- 4 to 8 indicates moderate risk.
- 9 to 21 indicates high risk.

SRSS: Externalizing Behaviors

Student Name	Steal	Lie, Cheat, Sneak	Behavior Problem	Peer Rejection	Low Academic Achievement	Negative Attitude	Aggressive Behavior	Total

SIBSS: Internalizing Behaviors

Nervous or Fearful	Bullied by Peers	Spends Time Alone	Low Academic Achievement	Withdrawn	Sad or Unhappy	Complains About Being Sick or Hurt	Total

Figure 2.1: SRSS/SIBSS screening tool.

Visit go.SolutionTree.com/RTI for a free reproducible version of this figure.

Staff who know students well can complete this screener at the conclusion of a school year. In middle or high schools, where teachers work with well over a hundred students in a day, the school can select homeroom or advisory period teachers to complete the screener, sharing results with colleagues to check for differences in opinion. In the absence of these types of periods, the school can dedicate one period within the day for teachers to complete the screener. Educators can use data from this screener to provide supports to students on the very beginning of the next school year, before another year of difficulties occurs. The screener takes little time to complete, and students with behavioral needs above a given threshold will very likely require immediate, positive, and structured behavioral supports at the start of the following year to be successful. The research behind these screeners specifies a "score," or "threshold," above which a student is deemed to be at risk for difficulties with externalizing or internalizing behaviors (a score of 9 or above corresponds with high risk). In my experience, there are often more students identified as "high risk" than is practically possible to support. In this case, the school may decide to raise the threshold above which students are provided with proactive and positive supports, with other students below this threshold on a watchlist. The term *positive supports* is important. We are not screening to prejudge or to prepunish but to prepare positive supports and environments in which we can preclude the difficulties that the screener predicts are possible.

Some students who experience difficulty accessing content and benefitting from instruction within the core Tier 1 environment may have health, nutrition, sleep, exercise, and sensory needs that are not being met. These skills represent coping strategies for stressors that, when lacking, will impede student success. We as teachers are unable to provide all of these basic needs, and, indeed, educators have not historically been trained or expected to know about cognitive or precognitive self-regulation. Consequently, and understandably, we may not even be used to recognizing deficits in these most basic and critical of foundations. Proactively screening for students with these needs is a first step in organizing and providing supports.

Importantly, screeners are not intended to diagnose or determine the causes of student needs or suggest the types of supports that are required to meet student needs. Diagnosing student needs is a separate step and set of processes, and will be described in chapter 3 (page 59) and much more extensively in chapter 4 (page 93). The SRSS and SIBSS are holistic screeners; the accumulation of points across the seven indicators within each screener indicates risk, but an elevated score on a single indicator does not necessarily equate to a diagnosis.

Transition Guides

As an alternative to the SRSS and SIBSS, teams of educators can systematically, consistently, and proactively reflect on student successes and challenges. For example, within K–8 schools in Chicago, Illinois, in which I worked, teacher teams collaboratively completed transition guides such as the one in figure 2.2 (page 44) at the conclusion of the school year. One of these schools was profiled in a chapter in *It's About Time: Planning Interventions and Extensions in Elementary School* (Weber, 2015b). The teacher team shared information from this chart with the next grade level's team of teachers so that it could proactively prepare positive supports that would ensure that students got off to a great start to the year. In addition, they shared this information with leadership and student study teams so that those teams could proactively prepare more intensive support plans for students with the greatest need in a timely manner, plans that would be initiated at the very beginning of the next school year. The school principal and leadership team provided the time for this important work and facilitated the process so that current teachers were empowered to inform their colleagues and so that the next year's teachers were empowered to proactively and positively prepare.

End-of-Year or Grade-to-Grade Transition Guide										
Student Name	Former Teacher (or Teachers)	Reading Concerns	Reading Effective Strategies	Mathematics Concerns	Mathematics Effective Strategies	Writing Concerns	Writing Effective Strategies	Behavior Concerns	Behavior Effective Strategies

Figure 2.2: End-of-year or grade-to-grade transition guide.

Visit **go.SolutionTree.com/RTI** *for a free reproducible version of this figure.*

When screening identifies a student to likely be in need of specialized supports so that he or she can meet the clearly defined behavioral expectations, there are two next steps.

1. Teacher teams collaboratively prepare differentiated supports, strategies, and scaffolds so that all students can successfully learn within core, Tier 1 environments. We will describe these differentiated supports in great detail in the following section.

2. RTI teams collaboratively determine the *why* behind students' difficulties with behavioral skills and design appropriate plans (perhaps Tier 2 or Tier 3 supports) that will meet their needs and ensure their success. We will discuss this in greater detail in chapter 4 (page 93).

Modeling and Teaching Behavioral Skills

We sometimes hear from well-meaning colleagues that certain behaviors—like motivation—cannot be taught; students either have it or they don't. It comes from within. This is simply not true. Consider this: we cannot teach "reading." Instead we teach students to identify the forty-four phonemes (sounds) within the English language; recognize initial sounds; discriminate sounds within words; make letter-sound connections; blend phonemes when presented with graphemes; attack words; read fluently (with accuracy, appropriate rate, and prosody); employ appropriate and high-leverage skills and strategies to comprehend what they read; employ appropriate and high-leverage skills and strategies to inferentially comprehend what they read; and much, much more. We don't teach students to read; rather, we model, teach, nurture, and reinforce students to independently employ strategies intended to ensure that they can make meaning of what they read. Similarly, we do not teach motivation. We model, teach, and nurture skills (such as mindsets, social skills, perseverance, learning strategies, and academic behavior) that enable a student to be self-motivating and engaged when learning, particularly when the learning process is uncomfortable or complex.

Student behavior is often the result of teacher-controlled variables. As a result, consistent practice and frequent modeling and teaching are critical. As Jim Wright notes:

> The toughest obstacle schools face in nurturing students' behavioral skills is to change the attitudes of teachers. When students misbehave, they are viewed as independent actors with total control over those maladaptive behaviors. In truth, however, those students are more likely to act out in response to classroom influences: they try to escape or avoid difficult work, are bored with instruction, or desperately try to manage their image in peer interactions. Teachers control important variables in the classroom environment. We need to bring all staff to an acceptance of this simple fact: Students don't 'fix' themselves. Students' behavior changes only when teachers' behavior changes. (J. Wright, personal communication, May 23, 2017)

We suggest that behavioral skills will flourish when pedagogies and practices ensure that behavioral skills are inextricably embedded into the fabric of all teaching and learning (Carr et al., 2002).

How can we as educators manage this responsibility? It will require that we reimagine the learning outcomes that we expect all students to meet, but it's worth it. A reimagination of essential outcomes will require us to think beyond student mastery of academic skills—those skills that are assessed on high-stakes tests—to also prioritize student learning of behavioral skills. Instead of only expecting third-grade students to develop a conceptual and procedural understanding of multiplication and division, we need to complement this important priority with an expectation that third-grade students further their development of positive mindsets, social skills, learning strategies, perseverance, and academic behaviors. Deep levels of student learning of both academic and behavioral skills require more than well-defined and articulated priorities. We must also continuously improve our pedagogies and adapt strategies to student needs. This section will focus on four teaching and modeling strategies for readers to use:

1. Identifying strategies for Tier 1 instruction

2. Finding time for instruction

3. Adapting instruction to improve mindsets

4. Focusing on self skills

Identifying Strategies for Tier 1 Instruction

Let's apply the same effective, research-based thinking as we use in academic teaching to balanced instruction of behavioral skills. The following is a list of ten instructional strategies and examples for teaching students the behaviors and noncognitive factors so essential to success in school, college, career, and life.

1. **Explicit instruction:** Staff teach, model, authentically practice, and reinforce the behaviors they want to see students exhibit. Principal McCoy of West Rowan Middle School concurs, "I use an expression with my staff—'Told does not mean taught.' We do a terrific job of going over our expectations at the beginning of the year or when specific incidents occur but often neglect to repeat this" (D. McCoy, personal communication, June 6, 2017). Explicit instruction is a critical component of Tier 1 instruction, academically and behaviorally. Teachers will provide clear guidance on what behavioral skills mean and what it looks like to display them.

2. **Metacognitive modeling:** Staff demonstrate what appropriate behaviors look like and sound like, thinking aloud and allowing students to observe how successful individuals navigate and negotiate social and functional environments. Think alouds are a powerful and underused strategy. In thinking aloud in relation to behavioral skill instruction, teachers may talk through with students how they plan for the work needed to prepare for a lesson; this would serve as an effective model of an important learning strategy skill that students must put into practice when completing homework and studying for tests.

3. **Scenario-based applications:** Staff and students engage in interactive explorations of scenarios in which appropriate behaviors must be put into action. Staff and students can collectively problem solve, brainstorm ideas, consider options, check the viability of solutions, and describe the *why* behind an agreed-on answer. Teachers may reference a situation from the preceding week in which difficulties with behavioral skills led to challenges. For example, perhaps during group work in a U.S. history class, teams of students did not display the appropriate respect, cooperation, or empathy. This scenario could be presented to the class, and students could reflect what occurred and problem solve what should have happened.

4. **Problem solving:** Students and staff apply the same problem-solving processes that they use when applying their academic learning for academic performance tasks to behavioral situations. Perhaps the performance task for a behavior minilesson relates to a student who is having difficulty in a science class. Teams of students could problem-solve how the student could apply the skills of perseverance, adaptation, and self-advocacy to address difficulties, with the result of each student group producing an "action plan" that could be used.

5. **Student-constructed learning:** Voice and choice are critical to increasing relevance and engagement. Staff can assign students to choose a behavioral category or skill that represents a need or interest for each of them. Students can then describe a situation in which these skills are important (either within school or outside of school), then identify how these skills would be employed, concluding with an explanation of how they would support a friend in such a situation.

6. **Social and collaborative learning:** Collaboration among students and student communication of learning are so important. Learning is inherently a social process. Blending individual explorations of behavioral skills with group work—just as we should with academic learning—is vital. Small-group and individual practice are both important. Staff can present challenges to small groups and individuals, asking them to communicate their thinking and produce their answers in various forms—orally, in writing, on video, through live demonstrations, and visually or graphically.

7. **Study examples:** Staff and students analyze positive and appropriate answers to behavioral scenarios, reflecting on why the solution is successful and considering other positive alternatives. A key strategy when engaged in academic learning is studying examples, such as a well-written essay, to draw conclusions on how to improve one's own writing. This strategy can be applied to behavior as well. Students can analyze an adult or student who employed, for example, effective self-regulation, self-reflection, or self-monitoring habits. The outcome of this study could be a commitment to using one related skill in the coming week.

8. **Study nonexamples:** Staff and students analyze inappropriate responses to behavioral situations, dissecting errors and generating answers that would result in better outcomes. This strategy is, of course, closely related to the study of examples, except in this situation, students are dissecting a *nonexample*, describing what happened and then what should have happened. Again, this strategy is regularly employed in academics, such as when a student is asked to explain the error made in a classmate's math solution, before correcting the error and solving the problem.

9. **Application:** Students apply behaviors and noncognitive skills to the tasks, projects, and learning situations that collectively represent the work they do in school. These assignments can serve as culminating projects, in which students draw on several weeks of behavioral learning to solve an open-ended problem, as we do in academics. The prompt could be: "A student's family has moved to a new city, and she is about to attend a new middle school. What behavioral skills and habits should she use to make sure she makes a successful transition? Refer to specific skills that we have discussed and provide at least three specific steps that this student should take."

10. **Check for understanding and immediate, specific corrective feedback:** Staff and other students provide feedback on the processes that led to answers. Students also self-assess their answers against a scoring guide that has been co-created and explained, and engage in the frequent (if not continual) revision and improvement of solutions. As with academic learning, assessment has the power to inform learning and can even serve *as* learning. Ask students to reflect on one behavior that they could have done better with in the preceding week, and give them time to share their responses with a partner. Encourage the partner to ask what the student would do differently and to respectfully suggest a strategy that has worked for him or her or a friend.

In addition, staff can employ periodic schoolwide assemblies devoted to clarifying consistent school-wide behavior expectations, and work together to design minilessons to employ during classroom meetings (described in further detail in Finding Time for Instruction, page 48). I recommend a greater commitment to establishing communitywide, shared expectations and nurturing genuine relationships during the first six weeks of school. In addition, I believe educators should:

- Increasingly engage in dual-purpose instruction—embedding behavioral instruction within academic instruction, and constantly and consistently reinforcing behavioral skills and noncognitive factors within the context of academic teaching and learning

- Involve students in the recognition and awareness of appropriate behaviors

- Regularly revisit and reteach expected behaviors every school day throughout the year

In other words, educators should employ the very same practices to model, teach, facilitate, and interactively engage with behavioral skills as we employ when teaching academic subjects like reading and mathematics.

Finding Time for Instruction

Staff might ask *when* they should teach behaviors. They might feel that their daily schedules are already jam-packed and that instructional minutes are at a premium. We are teaching behaviors all day, every day, whether we know it or not, whether we like it or not. If we don't proactively provide instruction on behaviors and authentic opportunities to apply these skills, misbehaviors will either inhibit student mastery of critical concepts and both academic and behavior skills, our successes in ensuring all students master prioritized skills will be less than we desire, or both.

So, when can we teach these behaviors? There are at least six opportunities.

1. **The first six weeks of school:** I have been embarrassed to hear from the teachers I work with that they have felt inhibited from establishing positive learning environments with students—with clear expectations, procedures, and routines, and positive relationships between staff and students—because they could not afford to get behind on their curriculum maps. Depth of learning is more critical than coverage of content. To combat this, I suggest revising the quantity of academic concepts and skills to be addressed during the first six weeks of school in acknowledgement of the time teams require to frontload the instruction of critically important behavioral skills and to build relationships. Teachers, teacher teams, and administrators with whom I have worked have found, after implementing this revision, that learning of all kinds has been much more productive the rest of the school year.

2. **Classroom meetings or minilessons:** Set aside ten to twenty minutes on a regular basis (once a week, twice a week, or once a day) to engage in minilessons on the behaviors and noncognitive factors that the school prioritizes (those it aligns, for example, to the scope and sequence of the curriculum suggested in the previous chapter, page 15), using the strategies for instruction described earlier in this chapter. Occasionally, these meetings can occur across classrooms or across the school. The Responsive Classroom approach, for example, suggests a daily morning meeting and a closing circle (Center for Responsive Schools, 2015). In the Responsive Classroom approach, teachers emphasize social, emotional, and academic growth in a strong and safe school community, and the sense of community is enhanced through morning meetings. In secondary classrooms, these may be known as restorative justice circles. These meetings may help you meet many important goals, including—

   - Setting the tone for learning

   - Establishing trust and building relationships

   - Motivating students to feel significant and competent

   - Creating empathy and encouraging collaboration

   - Supporting the integration of social, emotional, noncognitive, and academic learning

- Practicing metacognitive modeling, examining scenarios, studying examples and nonexamples, practicing skills, checking for understanding, and providing immediate, specific corrective feedback

3. **Behavior previews:** Prior to beginning a minilesson in mathematics, reading, or any other content area, remind students of one behavior on which you want them to focus—perhaps the behavioral priority that is a current area of focus within the schools' scoped and sequenced behavioral curriculum map. Or, engage students in a brief (ninety-second) preview of a behavioral priority prior to the transition to small-group work or prior to initiating a lab-like activity. Alternatively, ask teams of students to generate a list of two behaviors they should not see and two behaviors they should see within the upcoming brief period of teaching and learning. Call on students to share their team's ideas, validating or providing corrective feedback as necessary. Prime students to approach learning conscious of the mindsets and behavioral skills necessary to learn and grow at optimal levels.

4. **Behavior reviews:** Following a minilesson or other short period of teaching and learning, ask students to engage in a brief (ninety-second) review of less-than-appropriate behaviors that they observed (keep these objective; consider keeping them anonymous) and also appropriate behaviors (also keep these objective; consider recognizing the individual or individuals who behaved in a positive manner). Particularly when the practice of a specific behavior is less than optimal, consider revisiting the situation and the behavior during subsequent classroom meetings and previews. Carve out time for the reflection and feedback that lead to continuous improvement.

5. **Multiclass meetings:** Periodically, facilitate the same type of teaching and learning employed during classroom meetings across multiple classrooms, entire grade levels, or the entire school, or swap staff members between classes or groups of students. The consistency of explanations and understandings of the behaviors that the staff want to see and hear students display in classroom and non-classroom environments across campus is critical. Reinforce with students that it does not matter which staff member with whom they are interacting and it does not matter where they are—the expectations are the same. Furthermore, multiclass meetings allow staff and students to learn from and with their colleagues and peers—collaboration is powerful (Buffum et al., 2009, 2010, 2012).

6. **Within academic tasks:** Explicitly modeling and reinforcing behavioral skills during the completion of academic tasks enhances behaviors, engagement, and motivation. This will require that a positive learning environment, healthy relationships, positive beliefs, and clear expectations (procedures and routines) exist. The following are strategies and approaches to integrating behaviors.

   - Design and complete rich, rigorous, and authentic tasks that lead to deep learning and that require that students employ the behavior skills defined and referenced throughout this book. Students will learn academic concepts while they learn to fully participate and persevere in a task.

- Provide differentiated options and choices. Student engagement will increase as students explore an activity that they have selected, and their academic mindsets will be enhanced (for example, "This work has value for me" and "I can succeed at this").

- Require that all students complete a second draft of their work. Students will learn at deeper levels and demonstrate to teachers that they have mastered essentials and reflected, monitored, and persevered.

- Encourage students to try more than one approach and find more than one solution (if appropriate). Student learning will be more agile, and they will practice their adaptive skills.

- Foster a *not yet* approach to learning. Difficulties learning academic concepts will not be allowed to represent an impossible obstacle, and positive mindsets will be reinforced (for example, "My ability and competence grow with my effort").

- Include the requirement that students find and fix errors within tasks. Student learning deepens as they practice the skills of reflection, monitoring, metacognition, and perseverance.

- Reverse an outline from a sample solution. Students learn from and strive to model their solutions from an exemplar as they simultaneously learn to analyze and reflect upon their learning.

- Explicitly teach and require students to employ a specific learning strategy or set of steps when completing a task, such as metacognitive modeling, executive functioning, and self-regulatory strategies the staff have collaboratively defined and that the staff consistently use. Students complete an academic task while explicitly employing behavioral skills.

Adapting Instruction to Improve Mindsets

As we come to the end of this chapter, we'll revisit mindsets, those internalized student beliefs that so significantly impact other behavioral skills and academic performance. When students believe that they can learn, they tend to learn more and better than when they don't (Cheema & Kitsantas, 2014; Zimmerman et al., 1992). The presence of continual growth opportunities enhances a belief in the impact of one's effort on learning. However, our traditional instruction, assessment, and grading policies are entirely inconsistent with a growth mindset.

If we are to encourage a growth mindset in our students, we must move beyond instruction and assessment that disallow students to complete missing work and make-up tests. Instead, our instruction methods should be adapted to require that all students improve on their first efforts. English teachers have been providing opportunities for students to improve their writing for years; let's ensure that more of the tasks and tests that we assign to students nurture a climate of continuous learning and, once and for all, eliminate climates of fixed mindset habits for all students—those for whom achievement has traditionally been more challenging as well as those for whom it's come easy (Dweck, 2006; Dweck, Walton, & Cohen, 2014).

Additionally, the value of school from a student's perspective will improve when he or she sees relevance and purpose in the tasks that the teacher assigns. This will be possible when we substitute depth of learning for breadth of covering as many topics as possible. Racing through the curriculum compromises student exploration of rich problems, including problems of their choosing. Teach less, learn more, and improve student engagement in their learning.

A student's belief in his or her ability to be successful improves when frequent supports are in place to systemically meet student needs. Benjamin Bloom (1968, 1974, 1984) proved the success of exactly these supports beginning in the 1960s. Bloom called this *mastery learning*; in the 21st century, we call it Tier 2 of RTI. Using evidence from formative assessments, we must build in time to provide interventions and enrichments to deepen student mastery of essential concepts and skills. We must meet students where they are to deliver on the promise of high levels of learning for all.

Focusing on Self Skills

This is an appropriate time to describe the importance of, and our focus on, *self skills* such as self-monitoring, self-control, self-discipline, self-advocacy, self-starting, self-regulation, self-talk (metacognition), and self-critique. Our goal when teaching students to make meaning of what they read is not to comprehend for students. We as educators model comprehension, we guide students through the practice of comprehension, we assess comprehension, we provide feedback on students' proficiencies in comprehension, and we differentiate our supports for all students so that they successfully and *independently* make meaning of what they read. Our goal is that students display self-comprehension skills.

Similarly, behavioral RTI is not advocating that we behave *for* students. Our goal in nurturing behavioral skills in the ways that we have thus far described and that we will describe in the remainder of this book is to empower students to do these things for themselves. It's a gradual release of responsibility model, and we have not sufficiently applied these pedagogical approaches to behavioral skills in the same way that we have done with academic skills.

While Ryan Jackson notes that discipline rates are lower at his school, and student achievement and attendance improved, the benefits of modeling and teaching self skills are more relational. He says:

> Targeted goal-setting, where students and educators work hand-in-hand to both establish goals and commitments while also reflecting upon progress towards those goals through journaling, increases student confidence and their connection to school. Communication builds trust while garnering respect, both of which are imperative to improving and sustaining behavioral skills. (R. Jackson, personal communication, June 19, 2017)

The strategy of metacognitive modeling, or thinking aloud, described earlier in this chapter works particularly well when modeling and teaching self skills. Teachers can vulnerably and humbly articulate their own thought processes when thinking about a problem, and they can regularly acknowledge errors. In my experience, students not only want to be known by their teachers, they want to know their teachers. Thinking aloud not only models and teaches self skills, it helps establish positive relationships. Relationships are a key to nurturing behavioral skills, as described in the next section.

Nurturing Behavioral Skills

After teaching and modeling behavioral skills, educators must then nurture this skill development to ensure students' progression is sustained and enhanced. This section will present two ways in which educators can nurture student development of behavioral skills: through teacher-student relationships and through academic skills.

Nurturing Skills Through Relationships

According to personal experience and considerable research, strong teacher-student relationships lead to greater student outcomes (Allen et al., 2013; Baker, 2006; Battistich, Schaps, & Wilson, 2004; Berry & O'Connor, 2009; Hughes, Cavell, & Willson, 2001; Klem & Connell, 2004; Liew, Chen, & Hughes, 2010; O'Connor & McCartney, 2007; Reddy, Rhodes, & Mulhall, 2003; Wentzel, 1997). But how do we build, nurture, and sustain positive relationships within learning environments?

- **Let students get to know you:** Pedagogies and strategies matter, but students work hard for teachers they like. And they like teachers they know. Share a little about yourself—nothing too personal, of course, but appropriate and interesting facts about your family, your pets, and your hobbies. Incorporate this information into lesson and unit openers. Make learning relevant by connecting new content to your life. Educators typically really like what they teach, and we all have interests and passions outside of school. Share your enthusiasms with students, making connections to learning to strengthen relationships.

- **Teach students how to respectfully and productively cooperate and collaborate:** Students will always talk in class; the question is whether they will talk about what we want them to talk about or not. So, prepare students for meaningful collaboration by teaching them to have positive relationships. Give them sentence stems and starters for pairing with a partner and for working within teams, and practice these interactions. In my experience, even students who want to talk with their group partners aren't sure what to say. Stems may include providing students with language, such as:

    - What I am saying is . . .

    - I would like to say more about . . .

    - I would like to clarify my statement. What I mean is . . .

    - An example is . . .

    - What I said was . . .

    - I would like to add . . .

    - What I hear you saying is . . . .

    - Can you please repeat what [name] said, to help me better understand . . . ?

    - I heard [name] say . . . , which connects to [name]'s thinking because . . .

    - I agree/disagree about . . . My rationale is . . .

■ I would like to explain why I think [name] came up with that answer. I think . . .

■ I support/oppose this idea. My reasoning is . . .

■ We can and should expect students to know how to work with others in academic situations, and devoting time to modeling and teaching the ins and outs of empathetic exchanges will pay off. Student-to-student relationships are as critical to classroom and student success as staff-to-student relationships (Jacobs, Power, & Inn, 2002; Johnson, Johnson, & Holubec, 2013; Kohn, 1992).

■ **Get to know students:** Show them that you are interested. Listen. Hold them accountable—it shows you care. If and when you administer interest and preference surveys (and I recommend that you do this), use this information to prime both your academic and social interactions with each student. Play to student interests when designing lessons, writing tasks, and constructing questions. When greeting or privately sharing a fifteen-second exchange with students (see the following), follow up with a question about a club, sport, or hobby that the interest surveys mention. And, of course, use information from these surveys to differentiate teaching and learning.

■ **Ensure that every student receives a verbal message from you every day, or very nearly every day (and keep track):** There are students who can go weeks without adults at school noticing them—although many students like it that way. There is often one administrator for every five hundred students; one counselor (if there are counselors at all) for every three hundred students; and in secondary schools, a teacher can see well over one hundred students, perhaps closer to two hundred students, a day. Adopt techniques to interact with every student regularly: greeting students at the door with a handshake, high-five, or hello; interacting during fifteen-second quick-checks of last night's homework while students complete a warm-up; or by facilitating small-group learning opportunities within class. And keep track of these interactions to make sure that no student falls through the cracks. Maintain a check-off sheet that simply records that all students have received a verbal message.

■ **Initiate, re-dedicate, or revitalize advisory sessions, classroom meetings, restorative justice circles, or some combination, to building relationships:** Many schools have periods within their day when a primary focus of the time is as social as it is academic. This may be carpet or calendar time in early elementary grades, classroom meetings in the middle grades, or advisory periods within secondary schools. Make relationships an explicit goal of these sessions.

■ **Respect students' space and remember what it's like to be a student:** Active efforts on the part of adults matter, but sometimes students need space. And if we pay attention, we can tell when students are having a bad day. Nonverbal interactions matter, too. Eye contact, a nod, or a pat on the arm communicates to students that we understand and that we care.

What we say can enhance or compromise relationships. Our words to students sometimes unintentionally erode students' self-image, sense of efficacy, and mindset (Curwin, 2015; Curwin & Mendler, 1999). In figure 2.3 (page 54), the left column contains examples of words that do not promote a nurturing learning environment, and the right column provides more positive alternatives that encourage appropriate mindsets and behaviors (inspired by Curwin, 2015; Curwin & Mendler, 1999).

Do not say:	Instead, say:
"You have potential but don't use it."	"How can I help you reach your full potential?"
"I'm disappointed in you."	"What do you think you can do to make a more helpful decision the next time you are in a similar situation?"
"What did you say?"	Nothing
"If I do that for you, I'll have to do it for everyone."	"I'm not sure if I can do that, but I'll do my best to meet your needs in one way or another."
"It's against the rules."	"Let me see if there's a way to meet your need in a way that matches our school and classroom agreements."
"Your brother (or sister) . . ."	"We are all individuals . . ."
"I like the way Toby is sitting."	"Class, please sit down."
"You'll never amount to anything if you continue to . . ."	"I believe you will be successful, and I will support you to reach your goals."
"Who do you think you are?"	"How could you have been more respectful in that situation?"
"Don't you ever _____ (stop talking, listen, do your homework, try, care about your work)?"	What you feel directly
Anything sarcastic	What you feel directly
"I'm busy now."	"I'm very busy now, but you are very important to me. Unless this is an emergency, let's find a better time to talk. I really want to hear what's on your mind."
"The whole class will miss _____ unless someone admits to _____."	What you feel and need directly
"What is wrong with you?"	"I see we have a problem. Let's work together to find a solution."
"That's correct."	"Thanks! Do you have anything else to add? Does anybody else have anything to add?"
"You're so smart."	"You're making great progress! I've noticed how hard and well you've been working."
"You're a great artist (mathematician, writer, reader)."	"Your artistic (mathematics, writing, reading) skills are really improving. Why do you think that is?"

Figure 2.3: Examples of phrases that do and do not promote a nurturing learning environment.

Visit **go.SolutionTree.com/RTI** *for a free reproducible version of this figure.*

Students exhibit behaviors of all kinds, and educators expect positive behaviors, all day long across schools. No matter where the student learns, with whom, or at which time of day, we expect students to display appropriate and productive behaviors. Let's contribute to their success (and our success in serving students) by agreeing to nurture consistent expectations. The specific nature of a subject area or the preferences of a staff member rarely outweigh the value of consistently defined and reinforced behaviors.

Even elementary-aged students can interact with a half-dozen adults within a day when you consider the food service workers, campus supervisors, administrators, and other staff around the school. Secondary students may interact with twice as many staff members. We set up students or schools for failure when we expect students to appropriately navigate the rules of half a dozen to one dozen "bosses." Thus, ensure your staff agree on common general behavioral practices, in areas such as:

- Moving into the classroom
- Moving out of the classroom
- Using the restroom
- Using school tools and resources
- Correcting work in class
- Being tardy to class
- Missing class; absences
- Lacking the proper materials in class
- Turning in or collecting work
- Taking notes
- Presenting material; binder organization
- Asking questions
- Gaining assistance during independent/cooperative task times
- Grading
- Working collaboratively

In addition to nurturing behaviors through relationships with students, educators can also teach and support behavioral skills through certain academic tasks. This form of nurturing will be discussed in the following section.

Nurturing Behaviors Through Academic Skills

Certain academic tasks, requirements, and instruction techniques are able to simultaneously nurture behavioral skills that educators aim for students to develop. Many of these characteristics, in the following list, may seem familiar or like simple common sense. However, we believe teacher teams would benefit from referring to this list when designing learning experiences and from being disciplined and intentional when applying them.

The following are characteristics of instruction, activities, assignments, and tasks to promote positive behavioral skills.

- Educators facilitate learning as often as they direct it.
- Educators establish and practice clear expectations for students' independent and collaborative work.

- Tasks have multiple entry points and approaches.

- Tasks have more than one solution.

- Students have choice and can exercise voice regarding the specific tasks that they complete.

- Instructional expectations, standards, learning targets, and evaluation protocols are made clear to students in advance, and students seek the support they need to accomplish desired goals.

- Students and staff communicate clear, positive, confident, and high expectations for the achievement of all students.

- Educators expect that all learners stretch and challenge themselves, and they welcome challenges as an opportunity to learn.

- Students view mistakes as opportunities to grow, and they seek and receive specific *feedback*.

- Teachers and students value progress more than completion or a static, criterion-based grade.

- Educators prioritize questions as much as answers.

- Educators teach, value, and assess learning strategies (self-study, metacognition, self-regulation).

- Students learn from students.

Teaching behaviors must be a greater priority for schools. We must make the time within school days and periods of instruction for behavioral minilessons, and we must embed the teaching and learning of behaviors within the teaching and learning of academic skills.

Conclusion

The explicit teaching and modeling of behavioral skills must be a fundamental commitment and practice of all schools and educators. John Herner, past president of the National Association of State Directors of Special Education, said,

> If a child does not know how to read, we teach. If a child does not know how to swim, we teach. If a child does not know how to multiply, we teach. If a child does not know how to drive, we teach. If a child does not know how to behave, we... Teach?... Punish? Why can't we finish the last sentence as automatically as we do the others? (Elswick, 2018, p. 130)

We must commit to teaching and modeling these behavioral skills, just as we commit to teaching and modeling academic skills. The resources and steps outlined within this chapter will provide a foundation for the teaching and modeling of these skills.

Educators will achieve improving all students' behavioral and noncognitive skills neither through a program nor through reactive Tier 2 or Tier 3 interventions. Growth and progress occur when behavioral instruction, alongside academic instruction, begins within Tier 1 driven by collaborative teams of educators (Buffum et al., 2009, 2010, 2012). Within this chapter, I have shared a logistical, systematic process that staff can employ and that aligns to both Tier 1 academic teaching and learning and the supplemental (Tiers 2 and 3) supports that we can predict some students will need. We have deconstructed, reconstructed, and reframed those strategies inside of a new framework designed to support students in their learning journey—a journey that has no finish line, as we all continue to learn and grow, adapting to student needs and proactively improving students' self-monitoring, self-regulation, self-efficacy, and self-motivation.

There exists a strong case for the significance of the connection between academic and behavioral learning outcomes. This chapter has presented a framework for Tier 1 behavioral instruction that mirrors the approaches educators use to design academic instruction. It has provided strategies, supports, templates, and guides for an approach that supports behavior from a whole-child perspective, with an enhanced focus on behavior skills that support and enhance cognitive and noncognitive processes. This approach rejects the deficit model to addressing misbehaviors, instead building a foundation that reinforces students' academic and behavioral growth.

In the next chapter, we will discuss how we know whether students are demonstrating mastery of prioritized behaviors, what we do to provide feedback and support when they are not and when they are, and how we can proactively prepare for the differentiated needs of students.

Next Steps

The following are next steps for screening, teaching, modeling, and nurturing behavioral skills.

- Talk with staff about the purpose of screening and commit to efficient ways of gathering evidence about students most at risk. Be sure to establish the purpose of this screening—not to prejudge but to prepare a positive set of supports that a student needs to succeed.

- Make connections between the teaching and learning of behavioral and academic skills. Ask for a team to develop minilessons that all teachers can use during classroom meetings or social justice circles to support the explicit modeling, teaching, and practicing of agreed-on behavioral skills. Ensure that time is available and that the team receives permission for these learning opportunities to occur.

- Provide opportunities for teams and teachers to share examples of the ways in which they embed the practice and nurturing of behavioral skills into academic tasks. Consider videoing examples and engaging in learning walks, instructional rounds, or lesson studies on the topic of dual-purpose instruction.

- Commit to one way in which you and your staff will form relationships with every single student, and ways in which every student will be, and feel, connected to school. For example, you may aim for every staff member to know the names, interests, and needs of every single student.

Measuring Student Success, Providing Differentiated Supports, and Intervening Appropriately

In my world, there are no bad kids, just impressionable, conflicted young people wrestling with emotions and impulses, trying to communicate their feelings and needs the only way they know how.

—Janet Lansbury

In the previous chapter, we learned to model, teach, and nurture behavioral skills, both explicitly within minilessons and also as part of an integrated curriculum within rich academic learning experiences. We as educators must now discover how effective we have been in helping students develop these skills. We must know which students are successfully displaying these behaviors and which students require additional supports so that they too will develop these critical skills. We need to know with which behavioral skills students are relatively successful and those with which they need more attention. To do this, we must gather evidence and assess behavioral skills, just as we assess academic knowledge. Immediate and specific feedback and differentiated supports must follow this gathering of evidence. Data gathering and intervention correspond to the fourth through sixth steps of behavioral RTI:

4. **Measure student success in displaying these skills.**

5. **Provide differentiated supports that respect students' current levels of readiness.**

6. **Intervene appropriately and as necessary when evidence reveals the need.**

Within this chapter, I will describe how and when to gather evidence of student growth in behavioral skills via formative assessments and provide sample assessment items. I will then move to the important subject of feedback, providing qualities of effective feedback and discussing precorrective feedback. Next, I will discuss differentiation strategies for all students, including those who demonstrate mastery. Finally, I will present a case study of the follow up and follow through strategy.

Formative Assessment of Behavioral Skills

When we shine a spotlight on a priority, gather evidence about our progress, and celebrate our successes, all stakeholders appreciate the focus that we place on a given initiative. Schools have done this with academic skills in a variety of ways. Some schools create data walls, both for public and staff-only utilization. These data walls typically identify students within different bands of achievement as measured by regular benchmark assessments of prioritized concepts and skills within English language arts and mathematics. In the best of these situations, educators use these data to highlight students in need of support and, over time, display and celebrate growth by all students. All schools, in response to the No Child Left Behind Act of 2001 (2002) (if not sooner), have had their students' achievement in English language arts and mathematics publicly reported. For example, in southern California, all schools' achievement levels are reported on the California Department of Education website (cde.ca.gov) and in the *Los Angeles Times* (latimes.com). Whether right or wrong, fair or unfair, this reporting has focused schools' energies on improving students' academic achievement. This focus, particularly for areas that require more energy, is possible because schools assess students' mastery of academic skills.

We must shine an equally bright spotlight on student progress within behavioral domains. To meet this need, we must assess students' behavioral achievement. We cannot determine the extent to which students respond to the Tier 1 instruction of behavioral priorities if we do not assess their success in meeting expectations, and our success in helping them to do so.

This section will investigate the following topics relating to formative assessment.

- Formative assessment in Tier 1
- Examples of formative assessments
- When to administer formative assessments
- Progress as well as aptitude

Formative Assessment in Tier 1

Formative assessment and subsequent feedback are essential at Tier 1 because they can inform educator practice and motivate students to improve (Stiggins, 2006; Wiliam, 2016). However, the ways in which we have historically "assessed" behavior at Tier 1 have been inadequate. The evidence that schools have gathered on student mastery of behavioral skills (if they systematically gathered evidence at all) typically involved tracking student referrals to the office, detentions, or suspensions. These practices focused only on examples of difficulties in meeting behavioral expectations, and were quite delayed; evidence such as *Student sent to the office* or *Student went into time-out* does not provide staff or students with timely information with which to offer proactive, specific, corrective feedback.

Student and educator learning is best informed when information gleaned from assessments is specific, helpful, clear, and affirming, and helps draft a road map to how a student can improve (Stiggins, 2006). Assessing student progress toward meeting Tier 1 expectations can take various forms. The function is the same: to gather timely evidence of need so that teachers can provide feedback and make proactive course corrections.

Examples of Formative Assessments

In most respects, assessing behavioral skills is very similar to assessing academic skills. In both cases, assessment opportunities are frequent, efficient, accurate, tied to specific learning targets, and ideally used to inform future teaching and learning. Challenges that may emerge when assessing student mastery of behavioral skills will be largely mitigated when we design assessments that meet these criteria. Some might have difficulty finding the time to administer and collectively analyze results from behavioral assessments; this is a challenge we also face when assessing academic skills. We cannot know if students have learned if we do not assess. It is not enough to simply teach. We must determine our success based on learning (DuFour et al., 2016), and therefore we must gather evidence; we must assess. Some may experience challenges finding or designing assessments that they trust and that they believe are adequate. The following assessments and assessment processes will provide guidance, samples, and starting points.

We have had success gathering evidence through the behavioral equivalent of short-cycle academic assessments such as tickets-out-the-door, quizzes, and common assessments. To promote positive mindsets and behavioral skills, we strongly encourage that all assessments, including academic assessments, increasingly incorporate the following elements. They should:

- Monitor student *growth*
- Empower students to monitor their own growth
- Enhance student voice, choice, and agency
- Support self-assessment
- Involve error analyses
- Lead to immediate and specific feedback
- Inform future goals and action steps
- Provide multiple chances for students to demonstrate mastery of a concept, objective, or standard
- Differentiate for individual student needs so learners can show what they know, and so that we can *accurately* assess what we teach and intend students to learn
- Reflect mastery of specific concepts and skills rather than the average of points

The following is a list of specific examples and templates to utilize when assessing behavior.

- **Tier 1 assessment concerns:** See figure 3.1 on page 62 for a blank template and figure 3.2 on page 63 for a completed example. On a regular basis (for example, weekly), teachers or teacher teams share a summary of students about whom they have concerns, identifying with specific needs and providing a specific example.

- **Tier 1 assessment models:** See figure 3.3 on page 63 for a blank template and figure 3.4 on page 64 for a completed example. On a regular basis (for example, weekly), teachers or teacher teams share a summary of students who have exhibited models of behavioral learning, identifying specific needs and providing a specific example.

- **Student self-assessment:** See figure 3.5 on pages 64–65 for a blank template and figure 3.6 on pages 65–66 for a completed example. On a regular basis (for example, weekly), students self-assess their progress toward mastery of behavioral expectations, setting one goal and identifying how they are going to reach that goal.

- **Observation guide:** See figure 3.7 on pages 66–67 for a blank template and figure 3.8 on pages 67–68 for a completed example. Colleagues and administrators make informal observations of behavioral skills within classrooms. (We keep classrooms anonymous, not specifying the classroom, but instead aggregating these data.) They don't note specific students in need. The specific behavioral skill they observe may align with the school's scoped and sequenced curriculum map of behavioral skills, as outlined in chapter 1 (page 15).

- **Teacher-student conferences:** See figure 3.9 on page 68 for a blank template and figure 3.10 on page 69 for a completed example. Teachers meet with students one-on-one or in small groups, similar to reading or writing conferences. Use the questions in the template to conduct student conferences at Tier 1. The conferences are typically one-part assessment and one-part guidance.

Behavioral Skills Concerns	
Area of Need	Students' Needs and Examples

Figure 3.1: Template for Tier 1 weekly evidence-gathering form—concerns.

*Visit **go.SolutionTree.com/RTI** for a free reproducible version of this figure.*

Behavioral Skills Concerns	
Area of Need	Students' Needs and Examples
Engage, believe, and belong	Jeremy lacks confidence. He often says he can't do the assignment or doesn't understand but when I probe more deeply, he does. He does seem to value school and see a purpose in the assignments. He doesn't have many friends, and I'm having trouble connecting or finding connections with him.
Respect, cooperate, and empathize	Jeremy is awkward with his classmates. He doesn't engage in age-appropriate verbal exchanges and seems to prefer to work by himself. He sometimes hurts his tablemates' feelings by what he says or does but doesn't seem to mean to or to realize that he has.
Persevere, adapt, and advocate	Jeremy gives up very quickly. When the learning environment is new or the task even slightly different than the types that we have practiced, he seems to shut down. I encourage all students to ask for assistance. Students are encouraged to ask their tablemates first, then raise a "question card" at their table next. Jeremy has not done either but instead sits quietly or wanders the room.
Regulate, reflect, and monitor	Jeremy's organization is poor. He cannot find his supplies (books, pencils, notes) when he has them and seems to lose them quickly when I provide them. I give students time to study with a buddy, but he does not seem to know how or to take advantage of this time. All students are expected to "code" their errors using our simple system and to make corrections to their work. Jeremy has not yet done either.
Attend, complete, and participate	Jeremy's attendance is poor. He has missed thirteen days during the first half of the year. When he is here, he rarely finishes classwork or participates. He just doesn't seem to care.

Figure 3.2: Example of completed Tier 1 weekly evidence-gathering form—concerns.

Behavioral Skills Successes	
Area of Need	Students' Achievements and Examples of Success

Figure 3.3: Template for Tier 1 weekly evidence-gathering form—successes.

*Visit **go.SolutionTree.com/RTI** for a free reproducible version of this figure.*

Behavioral Skills Successes Example	
Area of Need	Students' Achievements and Examples of Success
Engage, believe, and belong	Jonathan never stops trying. We have adopted the motto "Not yet" in our grade level, and Jonathan constantly adds "not yet" with emphases for himself and others and for me. The exit slips yesterday weren't what I hoped. When I shared with the class the next day that we needed to spend another day on an essential concept because we hadn't learned it well enough, he immediately added, "Not yet!"
Respect, cooperate, and empathize	Jonathan is a helper. He is very attentive to others' needs. He checks on his tablemates' readiness all the time. If they need a paper or have lost their place in a lesson, he notices and very quietly helps out. One thing I've noticed is that Jonathan assumes different roles within the groups he works depending on the other members of the group. When he needs to be a leader, he leads. When he needs to be a worker bee, he works.
Persevere, adapt, and advocate	Jonathan is a tenacious learner. He always comes in for help during tutorial if he has a question. He emailed me last week asking if he could come in for help because he knew he needed help with Learning Target 2.3!
Regulate, reflect, and monitor	Jonathan's notes are beautiful! He uses multiple columns and colors, which I haven't ever mentioned. Maybe he learned it last year. He often arrives a few minutes early to my class since his class right before is next door, and I've noticed him reading yesterday's notes several times. He made a Quizlet for the last unit test (I guess he does this all the time) and emailed it to the other students in the class!
Attend, complete, and participate	Jonathan personifies SLANT (Sit up, Lean forward, Ask and answer questions, Nod your head, Track the speaker) and whole-body listening, which our team has taught and emphasized this year. He is always the first to participate, although I must say that he typically "lets" his classmates share if lots of hands go up.

Figure 3.4: Example of completed Tier 1 weekly evidence-gathering form—successes.

Behavioral Skills Student Self-Assessment	
Rate your success in meeting behavioral expectations for each area of need, according to the following scale, and provide evidence that justifies your rating. 1—"I need a lot of support." 2—"I'm experiencing some success, but I've got work to do." 3—"I'm making good progress toward goals." 4—"I'm consistently excelling."	
Area of Need	Score and Evidence

This week's goal:	
Strategies to reach my goal:	
Supports I need to reach my goal:	

Figure 3.5: Template for Tier 1 student self-assessment.

*Visit **go.SolutionTree.com/RTI** for a free reproducible version of this figure.*

Behavioral Skills Student Self-Assessment	
Rate your success in meeting behavioral expectations for each area of need, according to the following scale, and provide evidence that justifies your rating.	
1—"I need a lot of support."	
2—"I'm experiencing some success, but I've got work to do."	
3—"I'm making good progress toward goals."	
4—"I'm consistently excelling."	
Area of Need	Score and Evidence
Engage, believe, and belong	3—I came in during tutorial to retake my last test. Even though I got an A–, I knew I could do better.
Respect, cooperate, and empathize	4—I was my table's resource manager last week. I made sure that we always had what we needed. Also, Alyssa is having trouble in class, and her grandpa is sick. I made sure that she had as good a week as possible in class.
Persevere, adapt, and advocate	3—Like I said, I came in during tutorial to retake my test. I also went onto Khan Academy to see how to complete the types of problems that were on Monday's homework using the link that you provided in Google Classroom.
Regulate, reflect, and monitor	2—I need help here. I'm having trouble finding my mistakes, and my notes aren't helping me study. I'm wondering if there's a better way for me to take notes and study for tests.

Figure 3.6: Example of completed Tier 1 student self-assessment.

continued ➡

Attend, complete, and participate	3—My attendance has been perfect this month, and I haven't missed an assignment. I've been tired because I've had practice three days a week lately, but I'm trying to stay motivated by reading the 7 habits (1. Be proactive. 2. Begin with the end in mind. 3. Put first things first. 4. Think win-win. 5. Seek first to understand, then to be understood. 6. Synergize. 7. Sharpen the saw) that we're using in all of our classes this year (Covey, 2014).
This week's goal:	I'm going to take better notes.
Strategies to reach my goal:	Mr. Johnson has a lunch bunch next week on Cornell notes that he said I should come to.
Supports I need to reach my goal:	Mr. Johnson is going to help me. I'm also going to ask my mom for a new binder and notebook.

Teacher Observation Guide	
Behavioral skills:	
Characteristics	Score (Rank the characteristics on a scale of 1 to 4, where 1 means not evident and 4 means consistently evident.)
The teacher's instruction or the tasks keep students attentive and engaged.	
The teacher specifically states behavioral expectations along with academic learning targets when introducing classroom tasks or activities.	
The teacher continuously monitors students' on-task and academically engaged behaviors.	
The teacher monitors student behavior—interpersonal interactions, discipline, and self-management.	
The teacher consistently provides specific feedback to students for appropriate or acceptable behavior, with periodic positive reinforcement.	
The teacher consistently provides specific corrective prompts to students for inappropriate or unacceptable behavior.	
The teacher treats students with respect.	
The teacher provides five positive interactions for each negative interaction.	
Students demonstrate appropriate behavioral and interpersonal skills when the teacher is providing classroom instruction.	
Students demonstrate appropriate behavioral and interpersonal skills when working in cooperative learning groups.	
Students are prepared and on task at the beginning of the instructional period or activity.	
Students demonstrate appropriate on-task behavior when working independently.	
Students are on task until the end of each instructional period or task.	
Students treat each other respectfully, and no students are subject to inappropriate, negative, or verbal abuse by another student.	

Students treat the teacher with respect and do not subject the teacher to inappropriate, negative, or verbal abuse.	
Students in the classroom are eager and enthusiastic about learning.	
Student misbehavior rarely interrupts classroom learning.	
Students about whom there are concerns:	

Figure 3.7: Template for Tier 1 behavioral priorities form.

Visit **go.SolutionTree.com/RTI** *for a free reproducible version of this figure.*

Teacher Observation Guide	
Behavioral skills: Attend, complete, and participate	
Characteristics	Score (Rank the characteristics on a scale of 1 to 4, where 1 means *not evident* and 4 means *consistently evident*.)
The teacher's instruction or the tasks keep students attentive and engaged.	3
The teacher specifically states behavioral expectations along with academic learning targets when introducing classroom tasks or activities.	3
The teacher continuously monitors students' on-task and academically engaged behaviors.	2
The teacher monitors student behavior—interpersonal interactions, discipline, and self-management.	3
The teacher consistently provides specific feedback to students for appropriate or acceptable behavior, with periodic positive reinforcement.	4
The teacher consistently provides specific corrective prompts to students for inappropriate or unacceptable behavior.	4
The teacher treats students with respect.	4
The teacher provides five positive interactions for each negative interaction.	3
Students demonstrate appropriate behavioral and interpersonal skills when the teacher is providing classroom instruction.	3
Students demonstrate appropriate behavioral and interpersonal skills when working in cooperative learning groups.	2
Students are prepared and on task at the beginning of the instructional period or activity.	3
Students demonstrate appropriate on-task behavior when working independently.	4
Students are on task until the end of each instructional period or task.	3
Students treat each other respectfully, and no students are subject to inappropriate, negative, or verbal abuse by another student.	4

Figure 3.8: Example of completed Tier 1 behavioral priorities form.
continued →

Students treat the teacher with respect and do not subject the teacher to inappropriate, negative, or verbal abuse.	4
Students in the classroom are eager and enthusiastic about learning.	2
Student misbehavior rarely interrupts classroom learning.	4
Students about whom there are concerns:	
I noticed that Elena had her hoodie on for part of the period until she was asked to remove it, which she did. This isn't typical. Charlie and Dylan do not seem to know what to do or how to do it when working in their group.	

Can you describe a situation that occurred recently where behaviors didn't meet school or class expectations? (Prompt or provide an example if necessary.)
Why do you think that happened?
Who was affected and how?
How could we have reacted differently?
What behaviors should we have seen and heard?
What can we do now and in the future to support all students?

Figure 3.9: Template for Tier 1 student conferences form.

Visit **go.SolutionTree.com/RTI** *for a free reproducible version of this figure.*

Can you describe a situation that occurred recently where behaviors didn't meet school or class expectations? (Prompt or provide an example if necessary.)
My group really wasn't working well together yesterday.
Why do you think that happened?
We really didn't know what to do and didn't understand the problem or how to do it, to be honest.
Who was affected and how?
We just started talking about other things and got too loud. I think we distracted other groups, and you had to come talk to us.
How could we have reacted differently?
One of us should have gone to the Solution Table or asked you for help.
What behaviors should we have seen and heard?
We should have done self-advocacy and walked over to the Solution Table. You should have heard us asking you what to do.
What can we do now and in the future to support all students?
Maybe we need a reminder of what to do when we don't understand and how to use the Solution Table.

Figure 3.10: Example of completed form for Tier 1 student conferences.

We sincerely hope that teachers do not view these assessments—these evidence-gathering opportunities—as a burden or as simply more testing. We simply cannot inform our behavioral supports and determine needs in the absence of evidence. What gets measured gets addressed.

When to Administer Formative Assessments

You might be wondering how and when these evidence-gathering opportunities occur and what is done with these data. Teachers in schools that have implemented behavioral RTI dedicate time within the classroom, typically toward the end of a class period or lesson on a Friday, to having students complete self-assessments while the teachers themselves record their observations. It typically takes teachers another half-hour to complete this weekly or biweekly assessment of student strengths and needs. Combining these data with observation data from walkthroughs, teacher teams should work within their collaborative teams to apply the learning or inquiry cycle, considering the following questions.

- Which students are meeting or not yet meeting behavioral expectations?

- With what skills are students experiencing success and difficulties?

- What explains the difficulties of students who are not yet mastering these important skills?

- What feedback and differentiation support (including tiered intervention) can you provide to students?

These teachers recognize the power of even more timely Tier 1 assessment opportunities. Many of us have employed *behavior documentation forms* (BDFs) to gather information on minor behavioral infractions that occur in class (see figure 3.11, pages 71–72).

This document is not meant to be punitive in nature but would highlight concerns or incidents with helpful details for all stakeholders involved. Additionally, such incidents would not result in a student being sent to the office but would provide timely information to which administrators and other support staff could proactively and positively respond. There are, of course, situations that would necessitate that students are immediately sent to, or, preferably, escorted to, the office by a staff member, such as serious physical contact, verbal abuse, or dangerous behaviors. In these situations, normal protocol should be followed.

Progress as Well as Aptitude

It is important to not only measure whether students do or do not display behaviors but also whether they make progress. As with academia, some students will simply need more time and practice to improve behavioral skills. As RTI trainer and consultant Jim Wright explains, "The larger, more universal goal that teachers would like to measure is whether a particular student demonstrates growth in the ability to manage his or her behavior independently. That is the terminal objective" (J. Wright, personal communication, May 23, 2017).

No matter how a student's specific behavior or behaviors might improve with adult support, the teacher is also interested in tracking success in gradually releasing responsibility to the student to effectively regulate their own behaviors across all settings and situations. Teachers may measure and monitor progress weekly using the tools previously described or daily using check-in/check-out (CI/CO) procedures, as described in the next chapter (page 93). We teach reading so that students can comprehend for themselves when we are not guiding their reading. Similarly, we teach behaviors so that students employ all the self skills (self-monitoring, self-regulation, and so on) when we are not with them and they are not with us. As Wright notes, independent application of these behavioral skills is the terminal objective. But we must teach first (J. Wright, personal communication, May 23, 2017).

The tools and templates in this chapter are not the only ways of measuring student success in displaying the behaviors so essential to school and life. When gathering evidence of students' learning of behavioral skills, David Dockterman, a lecturer with Harvard's Graduate School of Education and former chief architect of learning sciences for Houghton Mifflin Harcourt, suggests educators consider leading and trailing indicators of the success of any mindset-related interventions:

> Test scores will trail changes in belief and behavior. If students are more engaged in learning, you should see improved attendance, reduced disciplinary action, fewer tardies, more homework turned in, and so on. And if you've done a good job articulating and teaching the behaviors kids need to be resilient learners, you should see evidence of those behaviors in the classroom. (D. Dockterman, personal communication, July 5, 2017)

<table>
<tr>
<td colspan="2">

School BDF

Student name: _____

Staff name: _____

Date: _____

Location:

☐ Classroom—Whole-Group Instruction

☐ Classroom—Small-Group Instruction

☐ Walkway

☐ Library

☐ Restroom

☐ Playground

☐ Lunch area

</td>
</tr>
<tr>
<td>

Major:

☐ Abusive or inappropriate language

☐ Fighting or physical aggression

☐ Defiance, disrespect, or noncompliance

☐ Lying or cheating

☐ Harassment or bullying

☐ Disruption

☐ Truancy

☐ Property damage

☐ Forgery or theft

☐ Use or possession of controlled substance or weapon

</td>
<td>

Comments

</td>
</tr>
<tr>
<td>

Minor:

☐ Inappropriate language

☐ Negative language

☐ Disengaged, lack of effort, or lack of work completion

☐ Physical contact

☐ Defiance, disrespect, or noncompliance

☐ Disruption of learning environment

☐ Poor participation

☐ Uncooperative

☐ Inability to work productively and positively in collaborative groups

</td>
<td>

Others involved:

☐ None

☐ Staff _____

☐ Teacher _____

☐ Peers _____

☐ Unknown

Motivation:

</td>
</tr>
</table>

Figure 3.11: Example of school behavior documentation form.

continued →

Follow-up action or actions:

☐ No recess

☐ Conference with student

☐ Restorative practice _____

☐ Parent contact

☐ Privilege loss _____

☐ Time in office

☐ In-house suspension (_____ days)

☐ Out-of-school suspension (_____ days)

Return to classroom teacher.

Parent signature: _____

Source: Adapted from Buffum et al., 2012.

*Visit **go.SolutionTree.com/RTI** for a free reproducible version of this figure.*

We can, in other words, use data that we already have to measure the effectiveness of our behavioral supports, for both groups and individuals. Principal Derek McCoy reports that the best "data [are] from teacher and student surveys regarding their positive impressions of a change in how students are responding to other students and teachers" (D. McCoy, personal communication, June 6, 2017). The evidence you collect will motivate changes and inform your future teaching and learning of behavioral skills.

With great enthusiasm, we should recognize the critical importance of gathering evidence of and providing feedback on the behaviors that we *want* to see. The essential topic of feedback will be the focus of the next section.

Feedback That Empowers

Feedback exerts a powerful influence—either positive or negative—on learning and achievement (Hattie & Timperley, 2007). It is important, whether we provide timely, specific, and positively-oriented feedback to amend inappropriate behavior or to praise appropriately used skills, to ensure that our feedback has the highest likelihood of having a positive impact on the recipient. John Hattie and Helen Timperley's (2007) model of effective feedback is a common-sense process in which learning from evidence significantly impacts future progress. This model starts by ensuring that both staff and students are clear on where they're going—in other words, with clarity surrounding the key learning target and corresponding expectations. Both students and staff next ask, "How am I going, and where am I going next?" The simple language of this process makes it accessible; the clear path it describes (what we're trying to achieve, evidence of how much we're achieving it, and what we need to do to keep moving forward) makes continuous improvement very likely. Educators are well versed in using different styles of feedback to inform *academic* progress, whether through grades, comments on assessments, teacher-student conferences, or in-class informal feedback. Feedback can also powerfully and positively influence behavior (Martens, Hiralall, & Bradley, 1997; Milan, Parish, & Reichgott, 2006).

There are loads of opportunities to provide feedback. Feedback is provided when redirecting off-task behaviors within the normal flow of the class, when privately talking with a student when the class is working on a task, or after or outside of class to reflect upon less-than-desired behaviors that have previously been displayed. Feedback loops are a crucial element of a behavioral system of supports. Behavioral skills aren't simply compliant actions that the student exhibits to make a teacher happy; rather, they are committed, authentic, and engaged behaviors that represent high levels of student agency and involvement in their learning. It can take time for a student to develop these skills; we therefore have ample opportunity to provide feedback to facilitate their journey.

In laying the groundwork for effective feedback, educators must establish and continually reinforce a culture of mutual respect and commitment (among staff, among students, and between staff and students). Feedback should be a two-way exchange, from teacher to student, and student to teacher. Teachers should check for understanding (thereby receiving feedback from students) and provide feedback that responds to this evidence of learning and need. Teachers invite students to give feedback on how their teacher supported them within the learning environment. Because this is truly a two-way process, students develop a stronger trust in staff and will more effectively synthesize teacher feedback due to lower affective filters. Feedback and positive, productive relationships are inextricably linked.

This section will discuss the qualities that make feedback effective and introduce the powerful strategy of precorrective feedback.

Qualities of Effective Feedback

Feedback is a critical element of each tier of support. Within Tier 1, we start by clearly communicating to students the purpose of feedback, and we reinforce the growth mindset contexts of the school and classroom—just as we articulate learning goals, objectives, and targets for instruction. For example, a teacher may say, "We are going to talk about some positive choices you've made today, and also some behaviors that aren't contributing to our growth as learners. We will also come up with some solutions together. How does that sound?" This process can provide a structure for the classroom meetings discussed in the previous chapter.

When providing feedback to students in these situations, we apply *three Rs*—reflection, reteaching, and restitution. We reflect with students on what happened, what could have gone better, and what should happen in the future. We provide immediate reteaching of expectations and strategies to meet these goals. And, we agree on how we're going to make the incident right and achieve restitution, including apologies, service, consequences, or a combination of these.

There are a number of qualities that feedback must have in order to be effective. First, feedback must be timely. Two desired outcomes of feedback are to change misbehaviors and to encourage the repetition of appropriate and productive behaviors. Both goals will be better met when students receive guidance on what occurred (the behavior that was unproductive or positive), what should have occurred (when providing feedback on misbehaviors) or ways in which the behaviors helped the student and others (when providing feedback on positive behaviors), and steps that can be taken to behave productively in the future. Timely feedback should be private when correcting misbehaviors and either public or private when reinforcing positive behaviors, depending on the personality of the student (Bangert-Drowns, Kulik, Kulik, & Morgan, 1991; Pintrich & Schunk, 2002; Shute, 2008).

Additionally, feedback from educators must be specific and precise. We sometimes assume that because we have redirected a behavior previously that every subsequent redirection can be more indirect. This approach assumes that students understand the intent of our verbal and nonverbal cues. However, students learn to self-monitor and self-regulate at different rates; hence, we must be explicit and clear with our feedback, in addition to being timely.

When providing effective feedback, educators should strive to (adapted from Weber, 2015a):

- Name concrete, specific behaviors

- Recognize students immediately after a good behavior

- Be genuine

- Attempt to catch kids being good

- Avoid bribery

- Use positive words

- Focus on the behavior, not the student

- Convey belief in students

- Use direct language

- Use a warm but professional tone

- Emphasize description over personal approval

- Recognize progress

The preceding research, in addition to John Hattie's *Visible Learning*–related research (Hattie, 2009, 2012; Hattie & Timperley, 2007; Hattie & Yates, 2014) consistently supports incorporating these strategies when providing feedback.

Ultimately, the aim of feedback should be for the student to analyze his or her behavior and its consequences and to choose to modify the behavior in the future. Feedback without the expectation of corrective action is simply a waste of time. Before such learning and collaborative problem solving can begin, staff and students need to have a common understanding and agreement of the behaviors that are growth hindering, and why those behaviors are a barrier. The previous chapter (page 35) described ways in which this common understanding amongst staff and students can be achieved. To reinforce these behaviors, educators can employ the three Rs (reflection, reteaching, and restitution, described on page 73) when conferencing, either formally or informally, to provide feedback to students.

When determining the cause of student misbehavior, the teacher may elicit some insight on the student's thoughts by asking questions—for example, "Were you frustrated with not understanding the directions of the activity?" During this time, the teacher and students brainstorm some possible solutions and corrections.

Important considerations and objectives of corrective feedback include (adapted from Weber, 2015a):

- Stopping the misbehavior and re-establishing positive behavior as quickly as possible

- Maintaining students' dignity

- Developing students' self-control, self-monitoring, and self-regulation skills

- Helping students recognize and correct any harm their mistakes caused

- Demonstrating that rules help make the classroom a safe place where all can learn

- Focusing on solutions that address the causes of misbehaviors and support progress

- Preventing the negative behavior from paying off for students; putting the negative behavior on the road to extinction

- Positively reinforcing appropriate behaviors (at least temporarily) to make the problem behavior ineffective

When I employed these strategies as an assistant principal and a principal, I found that, more often than not, students reflected "accurately." They were able to identify what they should have done (usually with little prompting), and they would have selected a harsher consequence than I did. We do not want to monitor students' behaviors for them. We want them to self-monitor. Particularly when further feedback and follow-ups are completed in subsequent days, students' future behaviors are more positive and misbehaviors decrease.

Precorrective Feedback

One powerful strategy for improving behaviors involves the use of precorrections that educators can provide based on predictive patterns (Colvin, Sugai, Good, & Lee, 1997; De Pry & Sugai, 2002; Haydon & Scott, 2008; Lampi, Fenti, & Beaunae, 2005; Lewis, Colvin, & Sugai, 2000; Miao, Darch, & Rabren, 2002; Simonsen, Fairbanks, Briesch, Myers, & Sugai, 2008; Stormont, Smith, & Lewis, 2007). Elements of precorrective feedback include (adapted from Weber, 2015a):

- Identifying known triggers

- Compensating for triggers and problem behaviors

- Disrupting causes of the problem behavior

- Proactively preventing or interrupting predictable problem behaviors

- Anticipating problem behavior based on prior behaviors

- Disrupting behavior patterns

- Providing prompts and supports to set up and support replacement and desired behaviors

- Teaching alternative and desired behaviors that meet the students' need or the function of the behavior (Hattie, 2009)

Positive, productive, immediate, and specific corrective feedback is not new and is research based (Hattie, 2009). The incorporation of feedback by staff and students into a teaching-learning process leads to progress in student outcomes, based on a reduction in the number of behavioral infractions or an increase in the number of positive behaviors displayed, as measured through a check-in/check-out (CI/CO) system (Kluger & DeNisi, 1996; Mouzakitis, Codding, & Tryon, 2015; Trope & Neter, 1994). Just as in relation to academic expectations, students deserve feedback on their progress toward behavioral goals.

In the academic arena, educators also put measures in order to differentiate their teaching depending on the needs of the students. Differentiation is critical to the successful implementation of behavioral RTI, and it will be the subject of the following section.

Differentiation

Carol Ann Tomlinson (2014) defines *differentiation* as common sense:

> Teachers in a differentiated classroom accept, embrace, and plan for the fact that learners bring to the school both many commonalities and the essential differences that make them individuals. Differentiation classrooms embody common sense. The logical flow in a differentiated classroom is this: A nurturing environment encourages learning. (p. 4)

Differentiation in academics has been well defined, but we must also define and apply differentiated practices in the teaching and learning of behavioral skills (Sousa & Tomlinson, 2011). We can predict that some students will learn at different rates and in response to different approaches or strategies. Just as in reading, mathematics, or other academic areas, a variety of factors will necessitate that we prepare to differentiate instruction of behavioral skills at all tiers.

We can predict that a student with significant deficits in prerequisite reading skills may experience difficulties in making meaning of text that the class is using as a primary resource in, let's say, an eighth-grade social studies classroom. We are committed to doing whatever it takes to ensure that the student demonstrates mastery of the prioritized skills and concepts of grade 8 social studies and are confident that, in collaboration between staff and between students, this vulnerable student will be successful.

How do we as educators prepare for success in this situation? We begin by identifying that the need exists and determining (at least preliminarily) the causes of the reading difficulties. In this grade 8 example, perhaps the student has difficulty decoding multisyllabic words, so his teachers provide one of the following five scaffolds to assess that information.

1. Text written at lower Lexile levels that addresses the same social studies prioritized concepts and skills

2. Visual representations of the concepts

3. Opportunities to read grade-level texts with peers

4. Access to audio recordings of the grade-level text

5. Sentence and paragraph stems and other structured writing supports so that the student can show what he knows

Perhaps this student also responds demonstrably better to visual instruction and support, so his teachers are purposeful and prepared to provide visual cues and resources to accompany the auditory instruction that can oftentimes dominate classroom environments.

As an important aside, learning for the student in the preceding grade 8 social studies example, for whom decoding multisyllabic phonics is a difficulty, is impacted by a significant deficit in a foundational skill—

successfully decoding multisyllabic words, which is a skill that teachers expect students to master in the upper elementary grades. In addition to Tier 1 differentiation and access to Tier 2 additional time and alternative supports (as the evidence indicates the student needs), this student would receive explicit, intensive, and targeted Tier 3 intervention support in multisyllabic phonics to ameliorate a difficulty that is significantly inhibiting his ability to access text and learn. We will dive into Tier 2 and 3 supports in chapter 4 (page 93).

The preceding scenario is familiar to most educators, and we accept that differentiated practices will be necessary to support student difficulties and differences when attempting to master academic skills. We must make the same commitments and make the same preparations to support student difficulties and differences when attempting to master behavioral skills.

We can predict that some students will learn at a different pace and in response to different approaches or strategies. We must prepare to provide differentiated supports in the learning of behavioral skills just as we do in the learning of academic skills. Just as in reading, mathematics, or other academic areas, a variety of factors will necessitate that we prepare to differentiate Tier 1 instruction of behavioral skills.

- Students lack knowledge of immediate prerequisite skills—they will require some preteaching.
- Students lack knowledge of foundational prerequisite skills—they will require more extensive scaffolding to meet grade-level expectations.
- Students have different styles, interests, or modalities through which they best learn.
- We have evidence, through frequent checks for understanding, that students will benefit from just a little more time and a slightly different approach within the core environments.

Armed with our proactive, predictive knowledge, we can begin to prepare differentiation strategies to use with our students.

Differentiation Strategies

Educators are undoubtedly familiar with the following twelve research-based common differentiation strategies (Lane, Menzies, Bruhn, & Crnobori, 2011; Waters, Lerman, & Hovanetz, 2009).

1. Preferential seating
2. Adapted, personalized, or more frequent redirections
3. Adapted, personalized, or more frequent positive reinforcement
4. Visual schedules
5. Proximity control
6. Tactile and sensory supports
7. Repeated and more detailed directions
8. More detailed problem-solving steps
9. Multimodal instructional strategies
10. More clearly defined parameters, boundaries, and expectations

11. Retaught expectations

12. Preparation for student transitions

I encourage you to employ each of these strategies more systematically, more proactively, and more positively, as follows.

- **Systematically:** Use these strategies across the school, for any student, with common procedures, when evidence indicates the need; moreover, use these strategies with fidelity (the way to use them) and for a long-enough period of time for improvement to occur. (While twenty-four useful repetitions are necessary to solidify academic learning [Marzano, Pickering, & Pollock, 2001], one hundred useful repetitions may be necessary to solidify behavioral learning [Benson, 2012].) Practically speaking, *systematic* means that a student in need of scaffolded supports to succeed would receive that support in the same way throughout the school day, no matter the teacher or environment. And, systematic means consistent, both throughout the day and for as long as the support is necessary. When a lack of adequate student progress is at least partially the result of our lack of consistency and follow-through, then we as educators are a major contributing factor in this lack of success. Tactile and sensory supports, a preceding strategy listed for students who struggle with arousal state regulation (they may be over- or underreactive to sounds, sights, or touch), can involve students squeezing an object or rocking safely in a chair as they manage their behaviors. We would use this strategy *systematically* by employing such techniques across all classrooms, within all environments, and with all staff members. This would mean that all classrooms and staff members would have the necessary resources (squeezy balls or safe rocking-type chairs) and know how and when to support the student in their use. If a student benefits from this differentiated practice, then we all must use it all the time; it should be used systematically.

- **Proactively:** Screen to identify students whose skill needs may necessitate the use of these strategies and provide supports to students before they establish more entrenched difficulties and frustrations. Practically speaking, *proactive* means that we don't wait; that we provide supports as soon as we possibly can. Proactive approaches can be informed through two processes. First, screening completed at the end of last year or the beginning of a new year will identify students for whom behavioral skills represent a need. Proactive means that the new school year begins with supports already in place within all environments and that all staff members understand and provide the supports. The second opportunity to support students proactively is made possible by the analyses of evidence collaborative teams complete as described a bit earlier in the chapter. When the frequent analysis of data indicates that some students need a little more and a little different type of support to be successful, then teams and schools have the opportunity and responsibility to provide these supports as soon as possible. We would use sensory supports like squeezy balls or safe-rocking chairs *proactively* by beginning the year with these supports in place because we have screened that a student needs them to be successful or because they were used productively last year and we effectively communicated and transitioned from last year's teachers to this year's teachers. We cannot, need not, and should not wait to introduce differentiated supports that students need for success behaviorally.

- **Positively:** Let's avoid employing these strategies with reluctance and from a deficit point of view; instead, let's consider them as we would consider the use of differentiation strategies for reading difficulties and communicate a growth mindset. Practically speaking, providing differentiated supports positively means that we do not blame students or their parents for difficulties; rather, we accept, and even expect, that some students are going to need a little more time and an alternative set of supports to be successful. A positive approach also means that we expect these differentiated supports to work and that we believe in every student's ability to grow. We do not, alternatively, go through the motions of providing supports (that we do not expect to work) so that we can move toward special education assessment and placement. Last, positive means that we provide feedback, recognition, and reinforcement when students are behaving in appropriate, productive ways; we do not only provide feedback (punishment or consequences) when students do not meet behavioral expectations. Using the squeezy balls or safe-rocking chairs positively means that this strategy is normalized—it's normal that students need them and can use them. Such a strategy is not unusual, and it is not a punishment, as in, "If you can't settle down, you're going to need to use your squeezy ball!" The use of behavioral differentiation strategies such as these should be as normal as differentiation strategies that we use to ensure students successfully access text in a reading lesson.

It's inevitable that we will need to provide differentiated behavioral supports within Tier 1 environments for students to meet behavioral and academic expectations, so let's be ready. In the following bulleted lists (adapted from Weber, 2015a), I suggest a few research-based strategies that align to the five groups of prioritized behavioral skills described in figure 1.4 (page 27). As we will point out in the next chapter, educators can use these research-based strategies to serve and support students at any tier. While the list is not exhaustive, the strategies should provide teams with a place to start.

1. **Engage, Believe, and Belong**

    Educators can do the following to help students *engage* in their learning.

    - Teach students to be aware of their attitudes about school and motivation for learning: "Whether you think you can or think you can't, you're right."

    - Build in rewarding opportunities for social interaction.

    - Equip students to act as peer tutors.

    - Teach students to set short-term goals for individual tasks and assignments.

    - Use examples freely. Students want to be shown *why* a concept or technique is useful before they want to study it further.

    - Teach by discovery. Whenever possible, allow students to reason through a problem and discover the underlying principles.

    - Transform tasks into mini-contests.

- Co-construct "futures" with students, and teach students to place themselves in that future.

- Co-construct goals with students, and connect tasks—small and large—to these goals.

- Explicitly teach techniques for self-discipline.

- Make activities stimulating. Choose contexts that you think will appeal to students (for example, sports or fashion).

- Provide audiences for student work.

- Connect academic requirements to real-world situations.

- Give opportunities for choice.

- Use game-like formats to liven up academic material and engage student interest.

Educators can do the following to help students *believe* in themselves.

- Identify, describe, revisit, and build off strengths.

- Use praise and corrections carefully. Avoid antagonizing language.

- Set realistic performance goals. Then, help students achieve them.

- Place appropriate emphasis on testing and grading. Tests should be a means of showing what students have mastered, not only what they have not.

- Provide attention without praise.

- Provide praise and acknowledgement for all.

- Show honest appreciation. Use *I statements* to convey honest appreciation.

- Promote fairness and avoid exaggeration.

- Develop self-motivated learners. Encourage lifelong learning and learning for the sake of learning.

- Give positive feedback and reinforcement (a note home, for example) for students who exhibit certain behaviors that relay confidence, like sharing something with the class or volunteering a certain number of times.

- Praise students frequently when they exhibit confidence.

- Minimize pressures on students. Remove competition or social comparisons and revise grading systems.

- Appropriately acknowledge students for performance and growth.

- Avoid sarcasm.

- Teach students to identify positive attributes of various phenomena in themselves and in others. Model these practices.

- Engineer early victories. Ensure students taste success, and systematically build off these successes.

- Recognize students for improvement, and acknowledge the effort needed to learn … always!

Educators can do the following to help students make connections to learning, class, and school (to *belong*).

- Teach students to talk to an adult when worried about school. Teach students techniques for coping with worry.

- Validate what a student is experiencing. Normalize the feeling, identify a time when the student was able to have a hard assignment and complete it, and instill confidence in the student.

- Take responsibility for motivating students. Like it or not, students are constantly expecting and collecting feedback from their teachers.

- Assign a classroom job (for example, scout or materials organizer).

- Foster a supportive environment. Students do not perform or think well when they feel invalidated or threatened.

- Get to know students. Display a strong interest in students' learning and a faith in their abilities.

- Involve parents. Share all techniques with parents. Encourage them to reinforce.

2. **Respect, Cooperate, and Empathize**

Educators can do the following to model and nurture *respect* for others, oneself, and school resources.

- Teach students to gather data on their own behavior and guide them to reflect on frequencies and reasons behind the numbers.

- Create a crate of activities, academic and less academic, with which the student can interact for a defined period of time as an option that they can select when they may otherwise disrupt learning.

- Provide two minutes of time with a teacher or peer when the student has successfully delayed his or her need for attention.

- Provide a second description of directions and expectations, thereby preventing predictable disruptions from occurring when a student should be working independently.

- Chunk tasks into smaller parts and have students submit their work to a staff member or another student before proceeding.

- When a disruption occurs, assign a written or graphic report, with or without stems and frames.

- Give positive choices. Structure requests to acknowledge the freedom to choose whether to comply or receive a logical consequence.

- Allow a student to save face; students sometimes blunder into potential confrontations.

- Teach *stop-walk-talk*.

- Assign a written or graphic report, with or without stems and frames, that addresses the incident.

- Teach and practice relaxation techniques to help students calm themselves.

- Provide, teach, and practice how to use replacement language.

- Provide, teach, and practice how to use guides that provide appropriate language as a replacement for pictured emotions.

- Design a simple inappropriate language rating form. Have students rate behaviors at the end of each class period.

- Direct students to state or write summaries of the incident and next steps, using appropriate language, as a form of restitution.

- Conduct a simplified functional behavioral analysis (FBA) (see page 121) that focuses on *why* the student is misbehaving—considering need, academic deficits, and physical or emotional anxieties.

- Project calmness. Approach the student at a slow, deliberate pace and maintain a reasonable distance.

- Assign a student at risk a responsibility-inducing job, such as serving as a scout. Scouts recognize students, at the end of a minilesson or time period, who have met classroom expectations, providing specific details.

- Ask neutral, open-ended questions to collect more information. Pose who, what, where, when, and how questions to more fully understand the problem situation and identify possible solutions.

- Praise (but do not embarrass), though use caution when praising defiant students. Ensure praise is sincere and specific. Ensure the praise aligns to the specific behavior and corresponding outcomes and does not align to teacher "likes" or preferences.

- Keep corrections and redirections to misbehaving students calm, brief, and businesslike. Sarcasm and lengthy negative reprimands can trigger defiant behavior.

- Use precorrection cards as non-verbal signals to remind students to perform their best.

Educators can do the following to teach and reinforce *cooperation*.

- Practice *I'm with you* statements, communicating empathy, acceptance, and understanding using students' own experiences.

- Assign older students to mentor younger students, even when one or both students displays behavioral challenges.

- Provide sentence frames to help students start conversations and structure deeper conversations.

- Teach and employ cooperative learning strategies.

- Use *Reciprocal Teaching* and other structures with assigned roles for students in a group.

Educators can do the following to model and nurture *empathy*.

- Explicitly teach *empathy* (the ability to understand and experience the feelings of others, and to respond in helpful ways).

- Model empathy. The best way to teach empathy is to model empathy.

- Meet emotional needs. Students are more likely to develop empathy when their emotional needs are met. Provide security; build relationships between adults and students, and students and students.

- Teach feelings identification. Label positive and negative feelings so that students can connect feelings with reactions.

- Get creative. Have students make "feelings" faces in the mirror with peers, and guess what each face represents. Share experiences with these feelings. Explain that you can experience emotions by just imagining them.

- Teach and assign responsibilities. Classroom responsibilities enhance empathy and caring.

- Teach problem-solving skills. Provide students with the opportunity and responsibility to solve their own problems, perhaps using stop-think-act.

- Listen actively. Project a sincere desire to understand and summarize concerns. Model the appropriate reaction to a difficult situation.

- Teach, reteach, or role-play strategies for using appropriate language in specific situations.

- Teach, reteach, or role-play strategies for identifying and respecting boundaries.

- Teach *cognitive restructuring*.

3. **Persevere, Adapt, and Advocate**

Educators can do the following to improve students' abilities to *persevere*.

- Encourage students to reward themselves for dealing with difficult situations well.

- Explicitly teach students how to create and follow a schedule.

- Chunk assignments, even assigning only one task at a time. For new material, trim assignments to the minimum length that you judge will ensure student understanding.

- Ensure that tasks are within each student's zone of proximal development, or the difference between what a student can and cannot do without assistance (Vygotsky, 1978).

- Explicitly teach, consistently reference, and ensure that students follow steps for success.

- Remove clutter from students' immediate work area.

- Frequently provide effective, constructive, descriptive feedback. Focus on decisions students make, not the quality of the work. Provide specific feedback that motivates and matures, not the label on the performance.

- Make every goal transparent.

- Display progress graphically.

Educators can do the following to improve students' abilities to *adapt* to new and challenging situations.

- Explicitly teach and model coping skills.

- Prepare an *emotional plan* with students. Role-play different situations and how students should emotionally respond.

- Provide the opportunities to use nondisruptive, tactile stress relief.

- Assign journaling and promote the practice as a healthy reflective tool.

- Teach, model, and practice self-talk scripts.

- Guide students in using a visual or written *Rating the intensity of emotions guide* to label and appropriately manage their feelings.

- Announce upcoming events and schedule changes in advance.

- Practice transitions from one activity to another.

- Regularly do a book-bag dump.

Educators can do the following to improve students' abilities to *self-advocate*.

- Ensure that students know how to access adults, and which adults to access.

- Teach and model how to ask specific questions.

- Provide opportunities for students to track their own progress toward mastery using evidence that they gather and that teachers provide.

- Ensure that opportunities exist within which students can seek and receive additional assistance, and be prepared to "require" students to take advantage of these opportunities until positive habits are established.

4. **Regulate, Reflect, and Monitor**

Educators can do the following to guide students in *regulating* their learning.

- Provide a quiet work area. When introducing these workspaces, stress that the quiet locations are intended to help students concentrate. Never use the area as a punishment.

- Avoid long stretches of instructional time in which students sit passively.

- Transition quickly. Practice transitions. Provide additional coaching to target students as they need it. Verbally alert students several minutes before a transition.

- Employ proximity control and assign preferential seating. Teachers focus instruction on a portion of the room; place the student's seat somewhere within that zone. Circulate the room.

- Provide frequent motor breaks. The behaviors of active students improve when staff permit students to quietly walk around the classroom when they feel fidgety. Alternatively, allow students a discretionary pass to get a drink of water or walk up and down the hall.

- Create motor outlets. When impulsivity involves playing with objects, substitute an alternative motor behavior that will not distract.

Educators can do the following to guide students in *reflecting* upon their learning.

- Teach students to connect new lessons and subjects to life and other subjects in school.

- Teach students to pause every few minutes to think about learning.

- Ensure that lessons and units begin and end with concrete, collaborative discussions.

- Model metacognition at all times, in *think-alouds* related to academic and behavioral learning.

- Teach students specific ways to review notes and new content.

Educators can do the following to guide students in *monitoring* their learning.

- Co-create advance organizers. Give students a quick overview of the activities planned for the instructional period or day.

- Teach students about self-assessing to ensure learning occurs.

- Teach students how to monitor understanding when reading and learning.

- Teach students how to prepare for classes.

- Create and reflect on *visual steps* with students.

- Adopt a schoolwide way of organizing learning, from binders to notes.

- Teach students ways to organize new learning.

- Explicitly teach students:

    – How to identify the most important information

    – How to use study aids provided in textbooks

    – How to create their own study aids

    – How to prepare for tests and how to create a plan of attack for taking a test

    – About different types of tests and test questions

      – How to reason through to an answer

- Model these strategies and allow students to practice.

5. **Attend, Complete, and Participate**

Educators can do the following to increase students' *attendance* at school and attention within classes.

- Conduct a simplified functional behavioral analysis (see page 121) that focuses on *why* the student is absent, considering health, emotional needs, academic needs, and potential bullying.

- Develop a plan to address the antecedents to absences.

Educators can do the following to increase students' *completion* of tasks.

- Match students' styles with pedagogy.

- Proactively and privately approach target students to reiterate and restate directions.

- Identify temporary positive reinforcers when students meet their goals.

- Provide students with a visible, tangible schedule.

- Increase the pace of instruction.

- Fully prepare and differentiate lessons.

- Use *think-write-pair-share* and related strategies frequently.

- Remove all items students do not need for tasks. Distractible students behave better when their work area is uncluttered.

- Select a peer who has a good relationship with the student and is not easily drawn off-task, and seek permission (from the student and parents) to appoint that student as a helper.

Educators can do the following to increase students' *participation* in their learning.

- Employ predictable structures, routines, and procedures.

- Reinforce auditory directions with pictures and other visual supports.

- Teach students how to collaborate, using cards or guides—with stems and frames—when necessary.

As noted previously, school teams should identify and define behavioral priorities that match their needs. Create a similar list of strategies and suggestions of all staff to use in providing differentiated supports to students for whom success is initially a difficulty.

Let's spend some time reflecting on the nature of the preceding strategies and ways to use them. These strategies have been curated from the most relevant research that we have found (Boynton & Boynton, 2005; Braithwaite, 2001; Brock, 1998; Carnine, 1976; DuPaul & Ervin, 1996; DuPaul & Stoner, 2003; Ford, Olmi, Edwards, & Tingstrom, 2001; Gettinger, 1988; Gettinger & Seibert, 2002; Heward, 1994;

Lanceley, 1999; Long, Morse, & Newman, 1980; Martens & Kelly, 1993; Martens & Meller, 1990; Mayer, 2000; Mayer & Ybarra, 2003; Powell & Nelson, 1997; Sprick et al., 2002; Thompson & Jenkins, 1993; U.S. Department of Education, 2004; Walker, 1997; Walker, Colvin, & Ramsey, 1995; Walker & Walker, 1991). In addition to being research based, these strategies are evidence based; my colleagues and I have used these strategies in our schools and have evidence that they work. There are no silver bullets, and there are no secret behavioral strategies that we've just been unaware of. Rather, these strategies seem like common sense. Let's commit to implementing them systematically, proactively, and positively.

Here's *how* we use these strategies: we gather evidence (through screening or frequent evidence gathering) that reveals to us that a student requires supplemental and alternative supports to be successful. We collectively analyze why we think the desired behaviors aren't occurring (or the function or purpose of the misbehaviors), and we target a specific skill to nurture and improve. Then, using the preceding bulleted list of strategies (beginning on page 79), we select a strategy that is proven to help students and staff improve the behavior; and we ensure that staff, parents, and the student know how to put the strategy into action.

Think of the way in which teams of teachers—collaborative teams—collaborate to make design supports for students in academic areas. The four critical questions of PLCs guide teams (DuFour et al., 2016):

1. What do we want students to learn?

2. How will we know if they have learned it?

3. What will we do if they don't learn it?

4. How will we extend the learning for students who are already proficient?

The preceding process of gathering evidence, analyzing the data, and targeting a behavioral skill, as well as the research-based strategies we suggest, help teams as they address the third question.

In my experience, I have heard colleagues express concerns over incidents within the classroom that escalate quickly and uncomfortably. We may be unconsciously and unwillingly responsible for escalating situations within Tier 1 environments. All adults within schools should study, practice, and employ the following research-based strategies to more successfully differentiate and de-escalate tense situations when supporting a vulnerable student with behavioral skill needs (adapted from Weber, 2015a).

- Create a safe, private, or semi-private environment for discussions.

- Limit the number of adults involved.

- Provide and protect a student's personal space.

- Do not corner the student.

- Display open, accepting body language.

- Speak respectfully and calmly.

- Use simple, direct language.

- Ask the student to take responsibility for moderating behavior.

- Provide safe, simple choices.

- Reassure the student.

- Provide an outcome goal.

- Identify the student's wants and feelings.

- Identify points of agreement.

- Describe an exit plan.

Remember—the researched-based strategies suggested here apply not only within Tier 1 but also within other instructional support contexts. It bears repeating: when educators employ research-based practices within the core classroom, we call this Tier 1 differentiation. When research-based practices are employed within the buffer or Tier 2 classroom, we call this Tier 2 intervention.

Students needing additional support are not the only ones who require differentiation; differentiation is also useful for enriching those students who demonstrate mastery. Next, we discuss techniques to help these students achieve their potential.

Differentiation for Students Who Demonstrate Mastery

Let's not neglect to provide differentiated supports for students who have demonstrated mastery of behavioral skills and who consistently display positive behaviors. The following are strategies that teachers can use in enriching student learning in these situations.

- **Allow and build the capacity of students to serve as peer mentors, peer tutors, and conflict mediators:** All students benefit from peer-to-peer supports, including students who have demonstrated mastery. Provide supports to students who may serve as mentors, tutors, or mediators and then give them opportunities to lead, analyze, empathize, communicate, and grow.

- **Recognize students who are meeting behavioral expectations:** This is a foundational element of PBIS, and yet there are schools that do not consistently or sufficiently recognize (in a ratio of five to one) desired student behaviors or that believe that rewards or extrinsic reinforcements of desired behaviors are bad. We do not, and have never, viewed positive reinforcement as a reward; we view and communicate these *caught-being-good* situations as recognition and feedback, as in, "Yes, thank you, that is an example of positive mindsets, social skills, perseverance, learning strategies, or academic behaviors." Some educators express concerns with the amount of time it takes to recognize students frequently in this way or concerns in keeping track of the practice. We recommend that educators consider getting other students involved. The concept of *student scouts* works well; these scouts provide specific feedback and recognition to students for positive displays of behaviors throughout or at the end of learning periods. Recognizing and giving feedback on behaviors need not be a controversial or laborious endeavor.

- **Without giving more work, nurture students' further development of positive behavioral skills:** For students who are highly skilled at demonstrating empathy, provide feedback so that these students continue to grow in this critical skill area. For example, when meeting with a small group of students with this characteristic, ask the group to think about what a student may be thinking when he or she feels frustrated or confused and what the group could do or say to help.

Behavioral supports are necessary and appropriate for all students. As noted in the introduction, behavioral skills are as critical to success in college and career as academic skills. We cannot assume that any student inherently possesses the mindsets, social skills, learning strategies, perseverance, and academic behaviors required for success in school, college, career, and life. In my experience, students for whom learning comes relatively quickly and easily benefit from an emphasis and prioritization on behavioral supports as defined in this book as much as students who have historically and unnecessarily struggled with learning academic skills and concepts.

Follow Up and Follow Through: A Feedback and Differentiation Strategy

I would now like to describe a specific technique that my colleagues and I have used at the high school, middle school, and elementary school levels to respond to assessment information, provide feedback, and differentiate behavioral supports for all students, one that leverages the behavior documentation form in figure 3.11 (pages 71–72). This strategy is known as *follow up and follow through*.

A prerequisite for this technique is a redefinition of the uses of, and reasons for, the BDF. This form is not synonymous with an office referral, which represents assessment data that are too late. When a student comes to the office with a referral, it limits our chances of proactively supporting him or her. A BDF, on the other hand, is typically completed when minor incidents occur. Students are not sent to the office when a BDF is completed (unless the misbehavior was of the major variety, which, after implementing behavioral RTI, we have found to be rare); instead, the teacher brings the form to the office at a convenient time once he or she completes it. Teachers may complete a few of these a day. The idea of follow up and follow through is that staff provide frequent, timely information on minor infractions and that administrative staff actively respond to the information within the BDF in a timely manner.

Students are not sent to the office at Shaw Middle School because Principal Jon Swett and colleagues:

> want to send two messages: First, the teacher is the boss and the most important person students need as their advocate. Second, students and teachers can and need to 'fix it' in a fully restorative environment—resolving challenges in the classroom keeps students engaged, and the administrative support team has a chance to support and model. (J. Swett, personal communication, June 19, 2017)

> **A Note on Sending Students to the Office**
>
> In matters of safety, a student leaving the instructional environment is totally appropriate. When safety is not a concern, the matter is complex, to say the least. The function of the student's behavior may be to escape or avoid whatever is occurring in the classroom. Leaving the classroom reinforces, even rewards, the misbehavior and makes it more likely to occur in the future. Moreover, this response teaches neither the misbehaving student nor other students in the class how to self-regulate. There are no easy answers, but there are answers. The differentiation, de-escalation, and restorative practice strategies this book suggests offer alternatives.

On receiving these forms in the office, the administrative staff would quickly enter the data contained within the form itself into a software system that efficiently captures the information and allows for simple analyses to be conducted when necessary. Then, no more than twenty-four hours after the teacher completes the form, administrative leaders visit the student within the classroom, ideally the classroom or time period in which the incident occurred. Administrative leaders do not call students to the office, thereby requiring them to miss class and providing them with the opportunity to take as much time as humanly possible to walk to the office. No, they go to the students. In addition to minimizing the amount of time students are out of the class, this timely follow-up accomplishes three things.

1. Teachers feel the support. They think, "Wow, the administrators are good to their word. I completed this form yesterday, and here they are to follow up. I'm going to continue to trust this process."

2. Other students notice. They think, "Uh-oh. They're here for that kid who acted out yesterday. They sure have high expectations here, and they hold you accountable."

3. The student in question receives timely feedback. He or she thinks, "Yikes. Here we go. I guess the staff here talk to each other."

On entering the class, the administrative staff ask to see the student, assuming that to do so will not be significantly disrupting the learning environment. They exit the classroom with the student, move into the hallway, and begin by furthering their positive relationship with the student (asking, "How's class today?" "How was the game last night?" "How's your brother doing?"). They then proceed through the *three Rs*.

1. **Reflection:** "Tell me what happened here" (while referencing the form).

2. **Reteaching:** "What should you have done? Oh, you're not sure; let me be clear . . ."

3. **Restitution:** "What can we do to make this right?" (Restitution may include an apology, an element of restorative practices, a consequence, or a combination of these.)

They conclude with the positive: "Hey. I know you're a great kid, and I know you expect more from your-self, and we expect more from you too. Please do the right thing, know that I'm here for you, and have a great, great rest of your day."

The administrators would write a date on the form that represents when they will stop checking in with the student: maybe they will only follow up once, or maybe every day for a week. When they communicate to parents, this is part of the information that they will share.

While this technique requires organization, and necessitates that administrators make getting out of the office a priority, this method of following up and following through is not difficult and produces many ben-efits in addition to those noted here. We believe that these timely, positive follow-ups prevent many actual office referrals for major infractions from ever being written. Early intervention is the best. We must, however, have data from efficient assessments; and we must do something with the evidence we gather.

Conclusion

Approaches have been suggested for assessing, differentiating, and providing feedback; now it's time for action. Transformation cannot occur until we apply researched-based ideas to schools and classrooms. We must close the *knowing-doing* gaps. Success will not occur until we recognize the significance of critical behav-ioral skills to students' short-term and long-term successes—until we enthusiastically accept the responsibility. Now it's time for us to act and collaboratively craft a set of supports for each of our unique contexts; it's time to build something transformative (Buffum et al., 2009, 2010, 2012).

We all want our students to live full, positive, and productive lives. And, we want them to thrive, succeed, give, connect, and change the world. Our society relies more and more on schools and educators to prepare the next generation of citizens for an increasingly connected and collaborative world. Our society counts on educators to provide every student with an education that nurtures both academic and behavioral skills.

All stakeholders, not only our dynamic teachers, must participate in creating and sustaining comprehensive learning environments. Leaders must equip and build capacities to guarantee that every student is on track to graduate future-ready. Like any new commitment, the development of behavioral skills must be continually promoted, communicated, supported, and refined as we progress through this journey. We can anticipate that all educators will need support in assessing, differentiating, and providing feedback in relation to behavioral and academic skills. Let's be ready.

The next chapter will describe why, how, and with what resources we create Tier 2 and 3 sets of supports for students. The foundation of Tiers 2 and 3 rests on the work of Benjamin Bloom (1968, 1974, 1984), who conceptualized and operationalized Tier 2 and 3 academic supports over fifty years ago. Tiers 2 and 3 rep-resent the additional time and alternative approaches that we can predict will be necessary for students to master the priorities of Tier 1. We will provide resources for:

- Determining why students are not yet mastering prioritized behavioral skills
- Efficiently diagnosing the antecedents, causes, and functions of student difficulties

- Determining behaviors on which we should focus

- Assigning strategies to support identified needs

- Implementing processes to monitor student response to these interventions

We will also focus on the critical concept of restorative practices, which can and should be a part of a school's behavioral supports at all tiers.

Next Steps

The following are next steps for measuring student success, providing differentiated supports, and intervening appropriately.

- Brainstorm efficient, frequent ways of gathering information on student success and student needs in relation to behavioral skills. Consider ways in which students can take the lead or play a significant role in this process.

- Dedicate time to providing feedback to students on their behavioral skill progress, and create or curate strategies, techniques, or formats through which to provide this feedback.

- Agree on a few proven differentiation strategies to use to support students with different behavioral needs. Practice these, collaborate about successes, and brainstorm revisions based on less-successful experiences.

Preparing for Tiers 2 and 3 Behavioral Supports

Only praise that places no judgments on a student's character or personality makes the classroom a safe place in which students are free to try and to make mistakes.

— CARLETTE HARDIN

We firmly believe that if educators consistently and effectively complete the steps that we have outlined in the previous chapters of this book, with high expectations in themselves and their students, there will be far, far fewer students in need of Tiers 2 and 3 supports. However, we know that educators will need to provide Tier 2 and Tier 3 behavioral supports to some students, so it is important to be prepared.

There are solid research-based and proven methods of supporting students' supplemental behavioral skill needs. We as educators can do a better job of putting these methods into action. This chapter will discuss how to appropriately and effectively provide, at Tiers 2 and 3, resources and processes for addressing the antecedents and root causes of students' difficulties. It will discuss questions to ask when designing behavioral interventions and determining students' specific behavioral needs for both Tiers 2 and 3. It will then provide tools for interventions at Tier 2 as well as resources for monitoring interventions until educators observe success. Afterward, we discuss interventions and monitoring within Tier 3, and offer templates for a functional behavioral analysis. Finally, the chapter concludes with a discussion of embedding the elements of restorative practices into the framework of schools' supports at all tiers.

Interventions at Tiers 2 and 3

Let's review what we know about Tier 2 supports, reviewing an academic example and drawing on the half-century of research-based, RTI-based Tiers 2 and 3 (Allington, 2011; Bloom, 1968, 1974, 1984; Buffum et al., 2015; Burns et al., 2005; Burns & Symington, 2002; Elbaum et al., 2000; Gersten, Beckmann, et al., 2009; Gersten, Compton, et al., 2009; Guskey, 2010; Hattie, 2012; Swanson & Sachse-Lee, 2000; VanDerHeyden et al., 2007). We believe that one reason why academic and behavioral RTI has been frustrating and less than effective in schools and districts is a simple misunderstanding of what the tiers actually are. Mike Schmoker (2004) observes, "Clarity precedes competence" (p. 85). Let's spend a brief moment revisiting the basic purposes of the tiers, paying particular attention to the least understood and implemented tier: Tier 2.

Tier 1 supports represent the high-quality, differentiated instruction—both academic and behavioral—designed to meet the needs of all students. Teachers help achieve this goal by collaboratively examining evidence of student response to academic and behavioral instruction and identifying which differentiated instructional strategies meet student needs.

When a student does not respond to this focused, differentiated core instruction, educators supplement *core* (Tier 1) instruction with *more* support (Tier 2), again whether the needs are academic or behavioral. Whether this means additional time or the use of alternative strategies or both, the evidence collected and the collaborative planning and analysis of all staff members drive supports. This is Tier 2. Decisions to provide these supports are based on evidence of a student's response to focused core instruction.

Tier 2 supports are fundamentally different than specialized Tier 3 supports. Simply stated, Tier 2 supports prevent students from *falling behind* or *falling further behind*, while Tier 3 supports provide the intensive supports necessary to *catch students up*. Tier 2 supports provide additional time and access to alternative strategies for more students to master more core priorities at deeper levels—we can predict that this will be necessary for some students. Tier 3 supports provide the intensive, immediate supports that students will desperately need when educators find significant deficits in the foundational skill areas of literacy, numeracy, and behavior to be inevitably contributing to frustration and failure—we can predict that this will be necessary for some students. In our experiences, most schools that have RTI-based systems of support in place are not offering *more* or Tier 2 supports to students. They are offering Tier 3, but their Tier 2 interventions are actually Tier 3-lite.

In actuality, Tiers 2 and 3 supports are distinct, and schools must move toward a future in which all students have access to both and receive both if the evidence indicates the need, along with differentiated core supports. The consequences of *not* providing Tier 3 supports are easy to imagine: students who are highly vulnerable due to significant skill deficits will become increasingly disengaged and will continue to struggle to simply perform as they currently are. But what are the consequences of *not* providing Tier 2 supports, even while providing Tier 3 supports?

Let's begin answering this question by acknowledging a reality: I do not know of any educators who have ever concluded a unit of instruction with all students achieving the depth of mastery that we desire and that students must attain. Likewise, we have never seen a classroom in which all students meet behavioral expectations in response to our first, best instruction. Students simply learn at different rates and in different ways.

What can we expect if, at the conclusion of a unit, we simply move on? Students will probably feel frustrated. In spite of the fact that the less-than-complete mastery of some priorities by some students was predictable, we have not prepared for this reality. Affected students' grades are negatively impacted. Their motivation for future success, their engagement, and their sense of self-efficacy diminish. The concepts and skills of many (if not most) subsequent units of instruction build on the concepts and skills of preceding units; this is even more true for behavioral skills. Students who have not yet mastered the preceding month's priorities and are not given an ongoing opportunity (or requirement) to do so will experience predictable difficulties mastering the next month's priorities. When this situation befalls a student unit after unit and month after month, we can predict that a significant deficit in skills will develop in short order and that a student's will to engage in his or her continued learning will similarly suffer.

Importantly and significantly, we have never concluded a unit of instruction feeling that we sufficiently extended the learning for students who have attained mastery. Time for Tier 2 supports can and should provide a service for all students: timely and targeted supports for greater levels of student mastery of academic and behavioral priorities, so that students don't fall behind (or further behind), and enrichment opportunities to engage with tasks and situations of greater complexity so students can reach greater depths of understanding.

Here's an example: suppose there is a student about to be in grade 7 for whom there are reading concerns. These concerns are known in a timely and efficient manner through universal screening; we examined assessment data that we gathered on all students (through regularly administered state [or province], district, or school tests) and systematically gathered input from teachers at the conclusion of the school year so that we had the information needed to proactively support students at the very beginning of the next school year. Let's say this particular student scored in the fourth percentile on regular administered districtwide reading tests. We do not yet know why, but there is something amiss, and we intend to do something about it. Moreover, this year's team of sixth-grade teachers notes that this student has difficulty reading grade-level material; they notice that he reads in a labored fashion and makes mistakes with longer words.

After universal screening and identifying that this student needs additional support, we must determine why this student is having difficulty. To do this, we sit with our soon-to-be seventh grader and listen to him read. Given that this student is performing at the fourth percentile (at least as one indicator measures), we do not ask him to read a sixth-grade passage; instead, we ask him to read a fourth-grade passage so that accuracy does not compromise our assessment of comprehension. While the student reads to us aloud, we listen for fluency (rate and prosody) and accuracy, specifically paying attention to any pattern of decoding errors. Following the student's reading, we ask a few comprehension questions. At the conclusion of this ten- to fifteen-minute period of informal diagnosing, we are in a position to confidently determine whether the student most needs (or first needs) targeted support in the area of single-syllabic phonics, multisyllabic phonics, fluency, or comprehension. We efficiently and effectively (albeit perhaps preliminarily) identify why the student was having difficulty reading.

Then, we determine what we will do to proactively target these needs so that the student is on the path to success. This seventh-grade team embeds buffer times within units of instruction and throughout the school year to provide intervention or enrichment depending on evidence of need that it gathers through assessments

(Tier 2 interventions). All students in the class will benefit from these buffer times, either from intervention or enrichment, and we can anticipate that our at-risk reader in this scenario may require these supplemental Tier 2 interventions from time to time. However, his needs are such that he is likely to require targeted Tier 3 interventions.

In an ideal environment, the school would have already developed a system of supports within which there are thirty-minute Tier 3 sessions in the various areas of reading difficulties, available within the school day. Assuming this to be true for our school, we assign this sixth-grade student to a targeted Tier 3 support that specifically addresses the most immediate area of need. Assuming that this situation is occurring at the end of the student's sixth-grade year, this intervention support would begin at the very start of the student's seventh-grade year. We would also prevent frustration and failure by being ready on day one of seventh grade with positive and proactive differentiation supports (such as text at the student's Lexile level, graphical and visual representations of key content, and audio versions of the course's texts) so that all students can achieve mastery of the course's priorities.

In addition, we would identify who on staff will take the lead in providing these supports and when the appointed staff will provide them, at all tiers. In this scenario, seventh-grade teacher teams would prepare for the differentiated and scaffolded core instructional supports that students with significant needs in foundational reading skills require to be successful in their courses. If a student cannot successfully read grade-level content, in the absence of scaffolded supports he will experience difficulties accessing learning. But all students can think. All students can problem solve. All students can learn. Educators cannot allow reading deficits to prevent students from mastering grade-level essentials. This student must have equitable access to meeting grade-level expectations as a result of scaffolded differentiation.

Last, we must ensure that we check on student progress frequently and accurately and ensure that we have a process in place for making necessary adjustments. There is no learning unless we know the extent to which students are progressing so that we can adjust our teaching. There is no RTI unless we know the extent to which students are responding to the interventions. So, to measure the extent to which our middle school reader who is at risk is responding to Tier 3 reading supports, we monitor progress in the skill area that matches the area of need, and the area in which we are providing support, at least every two weeks. If the student is receiving single-syllabic support, then we monitor progress in decoding single-syllabic words. If the student is receiving multisyllabic support, then we monitor progress in decoding multisyllabic words, and so on.

Additionally, we ensure that the RTI team (principal, administrators, counselors, special education staff, and teachers) meets weekly to review evidence to ensure that students—particularly students most at risk—are adequately responding to intervention. If students are adequately closing the gap, then we continue these supports until the gaps do not exist. If students are not adequately closing the gap, then we make adjustments to the type of support (or to how we are providing the intervention) until adequate progress occurs. No matter what. No matter how long it takes. Success is inevitable.

None of these practices occur in isolation, and they are not completed only for our fictional sixth-grade student. They occur automatically, systematically, as part of our specially designed RTI-based system of supports.

Questions to Ask When Designing Behavioral Interventions at Tiers 2 and 3

We as educators must prepare and commit to applying the same automatic processes we use in the academic arena for behavioral skills within an RTI-based system of supports. My intent in this book has been to describe what my colleagues and I have done, and what schools can do, to meet students' behavioral skill needs in the same manner as we ideally meet students' academic needs. We have had success in systematically and proactively responding to the following questions when designing processes and systems to organize our behavioral interventions.

- **"Which students are most at risk or likely to have a significant deficit in behavioral skills? Why is a student significantly at risk? What is the most immediate area of need?"** So that we can provide positive, differentiated supports within core classrooms and so that we can provide targeted, immediate, and intensive Tier 3 supports, we universally screen using processes and tools described in chapter 2 (page 35). Tier 2 supports can and should be informed on a regular basis using the common formative assessment processes and tools described in chapter 3 (page 59).

- **"Who will provide these supports? Which staff members are available and have received the professional development students require to administer these supports?"** Teacher teams take the lead on Tier 1 and 2 supports, both academic and behavioral. In our experiences, behavioral supports at all tiers also benefit from the involvement of a schoolwide RTI team. While grade-specific, content-specific, and course-specific academic priorities are largely distinct, behavioral skills are (or should be) consistent across grade levels, departments, and classrooms; schoolwide teams can help inform the types of behavioral supports that will most successfully meet student needs. Moreover, teacher teams are the experts in the skills, concepts, and content of their grade level or course; teachers may not yet have the same confidence and competence with behavioral skills. Schoolwide teams can help inform these supports.

  Behavioral supports are distinct from academic supports because, in most cases, academic supports are specific to a content area and can be targeted and practiced in small groups. Behavioral supports, however, occur within all environments in the classroom and across the school. It is also best to provide and practice behavioral supports within normal teaching and learning environments. So, who provides these supports? All staff do. Therefore, processes need to be in place to prepare, empower, and support educators in supporting students' behavioral needs.

- **"When will educators provide supports?"** Unlike Tier 2 and 3 academic supports, Tier 2 and 3 behavioral supports will likely occur throughout the entire day, within all environments. Behaviors can best (and perhaps only) be practiced within the actual, authentic educational environments in which they are necessary and within which they have not yet been successfully demonstrated. Educators need to establish preparations and systems to support both the staff who are assisting students with supplemental needs and the students receiving this help. There may be times during which small-group supports, particularly at Tier 3, are appropriate. One time may be when behavioral intervention programs, such as those described in table 4.1, are provided to groups of students with similar needs.

TABLE 4.1: BEHAVIORAL INTERVENTION PROGRAMS

Program	Behaviors and needs that are addressed
Aggression Replacement Training (www.aggressionreplacementtraining.com)	Physical respect and alternatives to aggression
Cognitive Behavioral Intervention for Trauma in Schools (CBITS; https://cbitsprogram.org)	Childhood trauma
FIRST STEP Next (https://pacificnwpublish.com /products/FIRST-STEP-Next.html)	Prosocial skill development
The Incredible Years (www.incredibleyears.com)	Social and emotional competencies
Check & Connect (http://checkandconnect.umn.edu)	Engagement, motivation, apathy
Anger Coping	Anger management

- **"What supports or specific resources or programs will best meet students' behavioral needs?"** The best intervention is a targeted intervention. The science behind behavioral skills makes this fact even more concrete. Students behave and misbehave for a reason. There are causes, antecedents, and functions that underlie behavior. Our task is to determine these factors and provide supports that address them and target the most immediate area of need. We provide tools and processes for determining needs at Tier 2 and Tier 3 later in the chapter (page 99 and page 119).

- **"How will we provide these supports?"** As with academic interventions, the relationship we have with all students, and in this case with our most vulnerable students, makes the difference between success and frustration. We provide supports with a combination of intensity, compassion, urgency, belief in students, belief in ourselves, and patient persistence. Success is inevitable, and behavioral challenges can successfully improve.

- **"How will we frequently monitor student response to this support and make necessary adjustments?"** Teams must make these decisions and develop plans that meet *student* needs and *staff* capacities. When monitoring the progress of a student receiving Tier 3 supports in the area of reading, one to two weeks is a frequency that we have used. It is both feasible to sustain and frequent enough to respond to information in a timely manner. We typically gather evidence of progress in response to Tier 2 and 3 behavioral supports on a daily basis, as described in Monitoring at Tier 2 later in the chapter (page 116). I recommend that data be gathered daily and more fully analyzed weekly.

- **"When will our RTI team (or leadership team, student study team, or problem-solving team) meet to analyze data, examine or re-examine student needs, ensure students are adequately progressing, and make the adjustments necessary to guarantee that this occurs? Are we meeting frequently (at least every two weeks)?"** Again, teams must make these decisions and develop plans that meet student needs and staff capacities. Six weeks is too long, in my experience; too much could have occurred in this amount of time that the team will not have had an opportunity to discover and address. Once a week has been difficult to sustain. Every two weeks strikes the right balance. Teams will be empowered to make timely adjustments, and the cumulative amount of time they meet will likely not be longer when meeting more frequently. Biweekly meetings will be shorter than monthly meetings, which will be shorter than meetings that occur every six weeks. And remember, teams need not discuss every student who is receiving supports and whose progress is being monitored. If a student is adequately progressing and responding to supports but continued intervention is still deemed appropriate, then staff should continue with the support. It's students who are not adequately responding (and students newly identified as in need of support) that teams should discuss, with the purpose of making adjustments that will improve the trajectory of success.

- ■ **"What evidence do we have that we're not only *doing* the interventions, but that they are *working* to improve student outcomes?"** Whenever a new student-improvement effort is initiated, we should ask how we will know if our work is resulting in improvements in student outcomes. Specifically, what will improve as a result of increases in students' behavioral skills? If a specific student at risk's mindsets, social skills, learning strategies, perseverance, or academic behaviors improve, what student outcomes will indicate improvement? We can gather anecdotal but valid evidence that habits directly associated with each of these categories are improving (for example, improvements in learning strategies are resulting in improvements in note taking and organization of resources). Improvements in learning strategies should also result in increases in work completion, increases in grades, increases in participation, and increases in attendance, and decreases in tardiness. What gets measured, gets done. We must measure the effectiveness of efforts; it motivates and sustains the efforts of both students and staff.

Addressing questions such as these—questions that we can predict and anticipate need to be addressed—is a critical preparatory step to providing supplemental supports to students in need. We can predict that some students will require such supports, and we must be ready. The next section will suggest tools that can provide school teams with the resources needed to be ready to meet these student needs.

Tools for Behavioral RTI at Tier 2

In chapter 3, we provided several tools and templates for identifying, in a timely manner, which students are not demonstrating mastery of prioritized behavioral skills in spite of differentiated core supports. See chapter 3 for evidence-gathering forms (pages 62–68), a behavior documentation form (pages 71–72), and questions to conduct student-teacher conferences (pages 68–69). Visit **go.SolutionTree.com/RTI** to download free reproducible versions of these forms.

Using one or many of these tools, complete figure 4.1 (page 100) within your collaborative team, teacher team, or data team to compile a list of students you believe are in need of intervention during predetermined

Tier 2 support periods. (Alternatively, use this form to compile a list of students demonstrating mastery, who are in need of enrichment in the same fashion.)

Data Source	Students
Evidence-gathering forms	
Behavior documentation forms	
Teacher-student conferences	
Other: _____	

Figure 4.1: Template to determine students in need of Tier 2 support.

*Visit **go.SolutionTree.com/RTI** for a free reproducible version of this figure.*

Once you have determined which students are in need of support, you must determine or diagnose the areas in which they need support and then apply a targeted intervention. These courses of action will be discussed in the following sections.

Diagnosing Areas of Need

We must then simply, efficiently, and accurately diagnose needs. Why do we believe the student is misbehaving or disrupting the learning environment? Figure 4.2 provides help in identifying student needs.

We do not need to be perfect in our analysis in figure 4.2, but we do need to know more about the characteristics of student misbehavior to help the student improve his or her behavior. The simple process described in figure 4.2, a process that a school administrator facilitates with input from other staff, can provide initial insights in minutes. We will undoubtedly learn more details about the student's needs once we start to intervene.

If more detailed information is necessary, then teams of educators can use the diagnostic interviews contained in figure 4.3 (pages 102–109) to further determine the area in which a student is having difficulty and the specific supports that would be appropriate. To gain useful information from these tools, teams of teachers and administrators should review the characteristics column, making notes when the needs described match the behaviors of the student who is being discussed. When the preponderance of needs is found to exist within a goal area, then that goal area likely represents the behavior that most, or first, needs attention and support.

Student name:
Clearly, specifically, objectively, and *observably* define and describe the problem behavior.
Identify the consequence the student receives due to the misbehavior. (Be honest, even if your response to misbehavior may not be entirely appropriate—for example, raising your voice or removing the student from the classroom.)
Specifically identify what the student seems to be seeking by misbehaving. Does this student seem to be seeking sensory feedback? Attempting to escape from a task or situation? Seeking attention? Attempting to gain an object or experience?
Describe how the student behaves immediately before incidents occur. Describe any and all behaviors, actions, words, or all of these.
Describe any patterns to the misbehaviors. Describe the environments, times of day, subject areas, groupings, assignment types (or all of these) during which the misbehavior is most likely to occur. What is the student doing or being asked to do? Where is the student? Who is the student with?
What alternative behaviors would staff accept on a temporary basis that may satisfy the student's need?
Consider administering a more specific diagnostic interview (for example, for attention or motivation), particularly if the student does not respond to initial interventions.

Figure 4.2: Template to determine Tier 2 behavioral needs.

*Visit **go.SolutionTree.com/RTI** for a free reproducible version of this figure.*

Goal Areas	Characteristics	Notes
Adapt	Worry and anxiety: • Worries about everyday things for at least six months, even if there is little or no reason to worry about them • Is unable to control constant worries • Knows that he or she worries much more than he or she should • Is unable to relax • Has a hard time concentrating • Is easily startled • Has trouble falling asleep or staying asleep • Seems stuck on a topic or issue • Restarts assignments repeatedly Melancholy: • Has feelings of hopelessness, pessimism, or both • Has feelings of guilt, worthlessness, helplessness, or all of these • Has persistent sad, anxious, or "empty" feelings • Displays irritability or restlessness • Shows a loss of interest in activities or hobbies once pleasurable • Has fatigue and decreased energy • Has difficulty concentrating, remembering, or making decisions • Falls asleep often • Complains of persistent aches or pains • Has frequent complaints of body aches in many areas (head, stomach, extremities) that have been investigated but not proven • Overeats or has a loss of appetite • Has thoughts of suicide • Is quick to react with anger or sadness • Often yells or shuts down when frustrated • Becomes frustrated easily • Requires lots of one-on-one attention • Has frequent emotional instability • Cries frequently over what appears to be small things (lost place in line, wrong answer) • Writes or tells of problems and reports in stories that they are upset • Frequently puts head down • Does little work or gives little effort • Has difficulty taking praise or criticism	

Goal Areas	Characteristics	Notes
Adapt	Bodily symptoms: • Has fatigue for no reason • Has headaches • Has muscle tension and aches • Has difficulty swallowing • Trembles or twitches • Is irritable • Sweats • Has hot flashes • Has nausea • Feels lightheaded • Feels out of breath • Has to go to the bathroom often Appearance and conduct: • Has red face • Appears flushed or tense • Has heavy breathing • Grimaces • Mutters or grumbles • Cries and refuses to work • Lashes out physically • Bites nails or lips, tugs at hair, taps feet or hands, or displays other nervous habits	
Attend	Attentiveness: • Daydreams—looks out window or around the room, looks past the teacher or other students • Draws or does other tactile activities while the teacher presents a lesson • Sleeps • Has difficulty completing assignments • Often fails to give close attention to details or makes careless mistakes • Is forgetful • Is frequently late Distractedness: • Plays with things in desk • Has difficulty sustaining attention in tasks or play activities • Often doesn't seem to listen when spoken to directly	

Figure 4.3: Observation checklists to determine how students are struggling and assign appropriate supports.

continued →

Goal Areas	Characteristics	Notes
Attend	• Often doesn't follow through on instructions, fails to finish schoolwork, or all of these • Often loses things necessary for tasks or activities • Is easily distracted Attention seeking: • Asks teacher questions that are geared toward being given the answer rather than seeking direction • Always needs to be around others to work • Needs lots of one-on-one attention • Gives many excuses • Has at-risk home environment (homeless, poverty, chronic illness, abuse) Attention to detail: • Has difficulty organizing tasks and activities • Often avoids or is reluctant to engage in tasks that require sustained mental effort	
Believe	Interpersonal skills: • Has difficulty making or maintaining friendships • Interacts poorly with others • Plays alone • Frequently argues or fights with others • Is unable to take a genuine compliment • Lacks friends Appropriateness: • Displays inappropriate behaviors • Makes inappropriate comments • Doesn't interact with other children in age-appropriate ways Emotional coping: • Displays emotions that are not appropriate to the situation • Exhibits perfectionist tendencies that interfere with social or academic progress • Is sensitive; easily has feelings hurt over little things or things that are not directed toward the student • Makes negative comments about self Self-discipline: • Rushes through work • Displays a careless, or unbothered, attitude • Makes big plans and then fails to follow through • Takes on more than the student can handle	

Goal Areas	Characteristics	Notes
Belong	**Connections:** • Is not connected to, or does not have a relationship with, adults on campus • Is not connected to, or involved with, a club, activity, content area, sport, or other part of the school experience • Appears to have a lack of support outside of school • Lives in an at-risk environment (homeless, poverty, chronic illness, abuse) **Follow-through:** • Gives many excuses • Fails to consistently follow expectations for work completion	
Complete and Participate	**Organization:** • Frequently turns in assignments late • Is disorganized • Turns in assignments completed incorrectly • Does not utilize an organization system • Is forgetful • Is unprepared **Self-management:** • Easily loses things • Experiences difficulty staying on task • Doesn't seem to know the directions or the content **Focus:** • Acts out or clowns around • Puts things off • Has a hard time getting started • Has no sense of urgency • Creates disturbances • Frequently has incorrect answers • Makes repeated, careless mistakes • Prefers to focus with intensity on one task when inappropriate • Has incomplete assignments **Learned helplessness:** • Blames others • Makes excuses • Excessively asks for help • Displays inability to work independently • Relies on others for help or for answers	

continued ➡

Goal Areas	Characteristics	Notes
Cooperate	Environmental awareness: • Speaks out of turn • Makes inappropriate or humorous comments at inappropriate times • Yells out Attention seeking or task avoidance: • Tries to engage others while they are working • Drops things, laughs, or makes noises on purpose • Claims to not know what is going on • Bothers other students • Gets out of seat frequently • Talks to others frequently • Throws objects • Makes noises • Rolls on the floor	
Empathize	Physical or verbal respect: • Has reports from other students of student verbally or physically harassing them • Bullies • Hits, kicks, or pushes repeatedly • Does not seem to realize he or she has hurt others, physically or emotionally Anger, emotion, and energy management: • Displays intense anger • Loses temper frequently or has blow-ups • Exhibits extreme irritability • Displays extreme impulsiveness • Becomes easily frustrated • Yells, screams, hits, kicks • Lies on the floor and refuses to do what the teacher asks • Runs out of the room • Runs around the room • Throws things • Pouts	

Goal Areas	Characteristics	Notes
Engage	Efficacy and self-efficacy: • Has trouble learning • Falls behind academically • Has a poor sense of self • Isolates him- or herself socially • Appears sad • Fails to turn in work • Has fears such as talking in front of others, or of failing • Has frequent absences or frequent reports of illness Inattentiveness or disengagement: • Has a short attention span • Displays varying degrees of boredom and indifference • Has a careless or unbothered attitude • Avoids activities • Needs to be frequently reminded to stay on task and to remember assignments • Has little facial or physical affect (often looks sad and unmoved by much) • Does not ask questions • Does not volunteer • Does not appear to enjoy school	
Monitor	Responsibility for learning: • Has difficulty taking responsibility • Has frequent incidents • Blames others • Brags to others • Denies when confronted Management of learning: • Frequently turns in assignments late • Turns in assignments completed incorrectly • Does not utilize own organization system • Is forgetful • Easily loses things • Has difficulty staying on task	

continued →

Goal Areas	Characteristics	Notes
Regulate	Physical regulation: • Often fidgets with hands or feet or squirms in seat • Often leaves seat in classroom or in other situations in which he or she should remain seated • Has difficulty going from point A to point B • Often runs about or climbs excessively in situations in which it is inappropriate • Often has difficulty playing or engaging in leisure activities quietly • Is often on the go or often acts as if driven by a motor • Pesters other students continually • Moves arms, shifts body, and plays with objects • Moves around a lot • Displays frequent pencil sharpening or bathroom use • Fidgets in seat or when standing • Has trouble keeping hands to self Verbal and emotional regulation: • Often talks excessively • Needs and seeks attention from everyone • Appears unable to control immediate reactions or to think before he or she acts • Often blurts out inappropriate comments • Shows emotions without restraint • Acts without considering the consequences • Finds it hard to wait for things he or she wants or to take his or her turn in games • Seeks constant assistance • Gives frequent excuses	
Respect	Interpersonal difficulties: • Lashes out verbally at others • Challenges the authority of adults • Has difficulty interacting with others outside of small friend group • Seeks to control friends • Swears or curses • Has frequent reports of inappropriate words or comments from other students or staff • Initiates verbal conflicts • Only makes negative facial expressions • Displays a lack of common courtesy	

Goal Areas	Characteristics	Notes
Respect	• Regularly so focused on a task that he or she does not notice others • Challenges the authority of the adult • Refuses to comply with adult requests • Refuses to follow classroom routines • Has confrontations frequently • Doesn't follow directions when he or she receives them • Frequently talks back to adults Self-respect and self-awareness: • Projects blame onto others • Talks about inappropriate things, makes sexual comments, or both • Conducts mature or immature discussion that is not typical of his or her age • Denies the obvious • Is unable to admit a mistake • Has poor judgment • Often plays out scenes of control • Asks the same question over and over • Is inflexible in his or her emotions • Exhibits a poor attitude • Does not think highly of others • Is often frustrated • Verbally states he or she does not care, does not want to do something, or hates things • Looks dissatisfied all the time • Talks back • Shows frequent anger	

*Visit **go.SolutionTree.com/RTI** for a free reproducible version of this figure.*

If educators desire even *more* detailed information, we recommend that teams use the more specific observation checklists in figures 4.4 and 4.5 (pages 110–114). In our schools and our experiences with colleagues from other schools, we find *attention* and *motivation* to be the most-expressed areas of concern regarding student behaviors, so the following observation checklists relate to the behavioral skill areas that include *attention* and *motivation*: attend, complete, and participate and regulate, reflect, and monitor. Readers may note that the categories within the following checklists may not seem directly related to attention and motivation; for example, self-confidence is a category within the attention checklist. Here's why: a lack of self-confidence may appear to educators as inattentiveness. When supporting to improve attentiveness in this case, teams should focus on improving self-confidence and self-efficacy. Difficulties with self-confidence and self-efficacy may be the cause of inattentiveness. Visit **go.SolutionTree.com/RTI** to access the observational checklists for the remaining three categories (engage, believe, and belong; respect, cooperate, and empathize; and persevere, adapt, and advocate). As with the preceding observational checklists, teams of teachers and administrators should reflect on a student's behaviors while reviewing the characteristics column. When the needs seem to exist within a specific goal area, then that represents the goal with which the student first needs support.

Characteristics of *attend, complete, and participate* The student exhibits the following traits.	Notes
Inattentiveness. • Does not complete tasks or jobs • Does not listen or pay attention • Daydreams a lot • Frequently requires others to look for things that the student has misplaced or lost • Has poor concentration on tasks that are difficult, hard, or boring • Often changes from one play activity to another, more than other students • Is easily distracted • Often makes us late • Makes others complete his or her work • After taking two hours to complete a twenty-minute assignment, loses the work or fails to turn it in	
Impulsivity: • Acts before thinking or considering the consequences • Changes frequently from one activity to another, more than other students • Has trouble organizing school work, doing homework, or turning it in • Needs a lot of supervision • Seems to be in trouble at school a lot • Interrupts others impulsively and blurts out answers in class • Has trouble taking turns in games or has trouble just waiting in a line • Has a lot of energy • Runs or climbs on things a lot, more than other students • Has difficulty staying seated in school • Fidgets a lot • Moves excessively during the day	

Characteristics of *attend, complete, and participate* The student exhibits the following traits.	Notes
Obsessiveness: • Gets angry when asked or told to do something different than what he or she is currently doing • Gets angry with change • Is easily frustrated • Is inflexible • Cannot deal with last-minute changes in plans • Won't stop asking for permission • Cannot take teasing from others • Will argue with staff even over small things • Always has to have his or her way	
Academic success: • Does not read very well for a student his or her age • Does not spell very well for a student his or her age • Does not follow verbal directions very well for a student his or her age • Has poor handwriting for a student his or her age • Takes a long time to complete work • Others complete the student's work just to get it done	
Anxiety: • Seems to be afraid of a lot of things • Worries about a lot of things • Seems to startle easily • Is easily embarrassed • Talks a lot • Seems to have to touch everything • Is nervous • Is often tense • Has trouble shifting from one activity to another	
Self-confidence: • Puts him- or herself down a lot • Is often negative about him- or herself • Seems satisfied with poor performance or grades • Does not like to compete with others • Gives up quickly • Does not seem to have much confidence • Does not seem to care about things • Seems sad • Cries or has tantrums easily	

Figure 4.4: Observational checklist for *attend, complete, and participate*.

continued ➡

Characteristics of *attend, complete, and participate* The student exhibits the following traits.	Notes
Defiance: • Is very stubborn—wants his or her way, and wants it now • Will not take "no" for an answer • Will not accept discipline, but will fight the teacher or run away • Always blames others for things that he or she did, and avoids responsibility • Lies rather than confessing to the truth • Rejects suggestions and must do things his or her own way • Is likely to cheat at a game so that he or she will win • Does not keep his or her word and breaks promises • Steals • Does not respect authority • Seems sneaky • Does not seem to demonstrate remorse	

Visit **go.SolutionTree.com/RTI** *for a free reproducible version of this figure.*

Categories of *regulate, reflect, and monitor* The student does not exhibit the following traits.	Notes
Metacognitive practices (knowledge and beliefs about thinking): • Applies school and skills to everyday life • Makes connections between new and old learning • Relates topics from one subject area to another • Rehearses learning with oneself and others • Identifies the skills he or she needs to make meaning of new learning	
Self-concept (seeing oneself as smart): • Believes in his or her ability to be successful in school • Attributes success on a test to effort • Confidently answers all test questions to the best of his or her ability • Believes that success is due to internal forces that are controllable, not external forces that cannot be affected; learned helplessness is absent • Believes that others will judge him or her as competent and confident due to effort	

Categories of _regulate, reflect, and monitor_ The student does not exhibit the following traits.	Notes
Self-monitoring (ability to plan and prepare): • Arranges and initiates steps for completing tasks • Assesses performance and progress toward goal • Establishes and adjusts work rate so that the goal is met by the established time • Quizzes him- or herself periodically to summarize and process learning	
Engagement (ability to maintain interest), for example: • Loves being in school • Studies all subjects with the same enthusiasm • Perseveres when work is difficult • Sets short-term goals • Spends time with friends and socializes only when he or she finishes work • Is driven to succeed, not to avoid failure • Pursues learning to grow and explore, not to earn points • Embraces mistakes as opportunities to learn	
Use of learning strategies (techniques for organization and memorization, including rehearsal and elaboration): • Makes drawings to help understand • Learns new words or ideas by thinking about a situation in which they occur • Translates new ideas into own words • Employs multiple strategies to learn new material • Prepares for tests with focus	
Volition (efforts he or she needs to stay motivated): • Keeps studying until finished even when the work seems less than exciting • Completes tasks with a plan and on time, not waiting until the last minute • Concentrates fully when studying, setting aside a length of time and sticking to it • Modifies learning environments to facilitate success and decrease distractions • Obtains and maintains the necessary materials and aids to complete the sequence and achieve the goal • Stops oneself from responding to distractors and delays gratification until achieving a goal	

Figure 4.5: Observational checklist for _regulate, reflect, and monitor_.

continued →

Categories of _regulate, reflect, and monitor_ The student does not exhibit the following traits.	Notes
Emotional control (techniques for regulating response to situations): • Views challenges and mistakes as normal and exercises strategies to manage stress • Seeks out trusted friends and adults to process stressors • Reasons through the relative significance of negative external influences • Attempts to identify the trigger for negative feelings • Considers other factors that may contribute to reactions to situations • Views tasks as opportunities to grow, instead of tests of self-worth • Adopts a task-involving orientation, with a goal of mastering tasks, instead of an ego-involving orientation, with a goal of performing better than others	

Visit **go.SolutionTree.com/RTI** _for a free reproducible version of this figure._

We do not ever use these diagnostic tools to determine what's "wrong" with a student or to pinpoint a deficit; rather, we diagnose to determine what specific support or strategy will target the student's need—to identify how we can help. As a team, use the preceding tools not as checklists but as prompts and guides as you identify needs and corresponding interventions.

Applying Targeted Interventions

The best intervention is a targeted intervention. Once teams have determined the specific behavioral skill areas in which a student requires supplemental support, it's time to prescribe a specific support. Figure 4.6 helps teacher teams create a plan that staff can put in place to support the student's development of behavioral skills. Many of the research-based strategies in figure 4.6 were shared in chapter 3 (see page 59). There is no difference between research-based strategies that educators can use to differentiate behavioral instruction within Tier 1 and research-based strategies that educators can use to intervene at Tier 2. I recommend that teams select a targeted strategy to match a support to a diagnosed need.

Let's work through an example. In this example, we will assume that the school has prioritized and defined behavioral skill priorities, and that they regularly teach, model, nurture, reinforce, and assess (gather evidence related to) student mastery of behavioral skills. Yet, in this example, there is a student for whom these Tier 1 supports are necessary but insufficient. This student regularly appears inattentive and infrequently completes work well or at all. Therefore, the student's teacher team provides differentiated supports within Tier 1. The teachers make an even more conscious and concerted effort to vary instructional strategies and modalities with the entire class and, very intentionally, for the student, and decrease the amount of time the student is engaged in a single task. After discussions with the student to prepare for the use of the strategy, the team of teachers begins to check for understanding with the student several times more frequently than with other students. Many of these checks are completed nonverbally, with the teachers and the student making eye contact and the student using a fist to indicate no understanding (regarding the content or the correct page, step, or problem

Steps to Supporting a Student With Tier 2 Supports	Notes
1. Determine on what behavior the staff and student will focus.	
2. Describe how the specific expectations associated with the target behavior will be retaught and by whom and when. • Utilize the instructional resources and minilessons that proved most successful at Tier 1. • Confer with staff who have had success with teaching the target behavior.	
3. Specify precorrections (see chapter 3, page 75) that have direct applicability to the target behavior.	
4. Specify de-escalation strategies (see chapter 3, page 87) that have direct applicability to the target behavior.	
5. Target an improvement strategy to the target behavior (see chapter 3, page 79).	
6. Build the student's capacity to use the strategy.	
7. Ensure that all staff can support the student with knowledge of the strategy and the plan. Support staff with any ideas, resources, or strategies that may assist in ensuring the student succeeds.	
8. Monitor the success using a *check-in/check-out* process (see page 116).	

Figure 4.6: Template to help staff support the development of student behavioral skills.

*Visit **go.SolutionTree.com/RTI** for a free reproducible version of this figure.*

number the class was working on) and five fingers to indicate total understanding. Precorrections are also used; teachers provide detailed visual schedules for the front of the student's notebook and teachers point to these schedules while they circulate the room. And yet, these differentiated supports do not result in sufficient progress and do not lead to necessary levels of success, as verified by evidence gathered by the teacher and school.

So, the team, with administrators' supports, more deeply analyzes characteristics of the student's behavior using figures 4.3 (pages 102–109), 4.4 (pages 110–112), and 4.5 (page 112–114). They determine that inattentiveness for the student was exacerbated by anxiety and a lack of resource organization. Guided by figure 4.6 (page 115), they agree to implement a more comprehensive set of supports: they teach the student positive self-task strategies and use these phrases with the student throughout the day. They also complete twice-daily binder and backpack checks during check-in and check-out (see Monitoring at Tier 2 on this page for more details on check-in/check-out).

Supporting students with supplemental behavioral needs—needs that are not being met within Tier 1—takes time, both to determine the necessary supports and to implement them. But this time is worth it: teachers and teacher teams are more empowered to effect change, individual student behavior improves, and teaching and learning for all are more productive.

Once your intervention is in place, it is essential to monitor the student's progress. Neither staff nor students will know whether progress is being made and whether efforts are productive if teachers do not gather evidence. And there's a bonus when monitoring the success of behavioral interventions: monitoring provides an opportunity for mentoring, strengthening relationships, and connecting students at risk to staff at school.

Monitoring at Tier 2

There is no response to intervention if we as educators do not measure the extent to which students are responding. Progress monitoring, and our response to the evidence we gather, are essential and are why RTI cannot fail: it's a self-correcting system. There is a research-based way to monitor and mentor students to behavioral success—a process that empowers educators and students known as *check-in/check-out* (CI/CO; see Campbell & Anderson, 2011; Hawken & Horner, 2003; Todd, Campbell, Meyer, & Horner, 2008).

It's critical to share an important point about CI/CO. While CI/CO has important monitoring elements, as the following describes, CI/CO is not a Tier 2 *intervention* for behavioral needs. The interventions within Tier 2 are the strategies that support a student's improvement in a specific behavior that was selected after an informal diagnostic process determined the need. CI/CO, on the other hand, is the research-based and powerful way in which educators *monitor* a student's response to a Tier 2 behavioral intervention; it's primarily a progress monitoring process and tool.

CI/CO supports students as they build better habits, including the habit of self-monitoring behavior. The following can occur within the CI/CO process (adapted from Weber, 2015a).

- Staff assist with frequent monitoring while better habits are built.
- The school identifies a CI/CO staff mentor—someone who has or is willing to have a relationship with the student—and he or she schedules times to check in with the student for

two to three minutes before school and to check out with the student for five to six minutes after school. See figure 4.7 (page 118) for possible conversation starters for CI/CO.

- Teacher teams establish and note frequencies for CI/CO monitoring throughout the day with relevant staff on the CI/CO form.

- Teams note on the CI/CO form the target behavior and related focus strategy.

- The student reflects on and rates his or her performance in relation to the target behavior on the CI/CO form at the conclusion of each time period the form notes.

- The student presents (or the staff prompt the student to present) the CI/CO form at the conclusion of each time period the form notes.

- Each of the student's teachers rates the student's performance in relation to the target behavior. Out of respect for a teacher's time, a debrief need not occur at these times; the CI/CO mentor will guide a thorough reflection on the day's successes and challenges at the end of the day.

- During check-out, the mentor and student determine daily point totals and award a reinforcement, if the student earns the goal.

- The student obtains his or her parents' signatures, which the educator will verify at the next day's check-in.

- Periodically (typically at the end of each week), the mentor plots daily point totals; the student and mentor reflect on progress and establish future goals.

All educators should have the opportunity to be an adult mentor who checks in and checks out with students in need. The only requirement is that they must believe in, and be willing to have a positive relationship with, students. To support staff in this role, I have collected a few sample questions and comments to use during CI/CO (figure 4.7, page 118).

Progress monitoring through CI/CO monitors both student progress and the efficacy of supports in a timely (daily) manner. Of course, the relationship and feedback elements of CI/CO matter as well. Jim Wright recommends that the:

> teacher and student meet to develop a behavior checklist, as the student's participation in making the checklist can increase motivation to follow it. I also like checklists as a low-key "precorrective": the student is prompted to look over the elements of the checklist at the "point of performance," just before they move into the challenging situation or setting where they are expected to show the positive behaviors that the checklist addresses. (J. Wright, personal communication, May 23, 2017)

Monitoring must occur so that educators and (more importantly) students know when progress occurs, and so that they can make adjustments when it isn't. Figure 4.8 (page 119) is an example of a CI/CO form. I encourage schools to use electronic versions of the form if possible. Each element of the form is important; fidelity to CI/CO matters.

At Check-In	At Check-Out
Mentors should say the following at check-in.	Mentors should ask the following at check-out.
• Tell me how your afternoon was.	• Can we take a look at your sheet?
• Let's remind ourselves of how many points you earned yesterday.	• Why do you think Ms. Harris and you disagree about how well you did in reading?
• Share one thing that went well yesterday.	• Can you tell me about that?
• Name one thing that could have gone better.	• What are you most proud of today?
• Share your goal for today.	• What could have gone better?
• Have a great day, and good luck on your [subject area] test.	• How was your mathematics test?
• See you after school.	• What are you doing after school?
• Nice! You brought your agenda for us to review!	• How many points did you earn today?
• You're here on time again. Great!	• What's your point goal for tomorrow?
• It's great to see you this morning.	• You're right on target. How can you keep up the good work?
• Looks like you're ready for a good day.	• You made your goal. Nice! How does it feel?
• You're off to a good start.	• Looks like today didn't go so well; can you tell me about it?
• You look happy to be here this morning.	• You look a little frustrated. What happened?
• I like the way you said "good morning."	Mentors can also say one of the following at check-out.
• Thanks for coming to check-in.	• You had a great (awesome, terrific, or something similar) day!
• Sounds like you had a good weekend.	• Your parent is going to be so proud of you.
• We missed you yesterday (if student was absent); nice to see you today.	• You're really working hard!
	• I know it was a tough day—thanks for coming to check-out.
	• We all have bad days once in a while; I know you can do it tomorrow.
	• Looks like you were having some trouble today. I know you can turn it around tomorrow.

Figure 4.7: Sample check-in/check-out conversation starters.

Visit **go.SolutionTree.com/RTI** *for a free reproducible version of this figure.*

Check-in/check-out for _____ (student name)

Check-in/check-out with _____ (staff member)

Date: _____

Today, I am working on: _____ (Target behavior with specific description if necessary)

Focus strategy: _____ (Strategy that matches target behavior)

This is how I did today:

- 3—Great! (I was reminded to be on task one to zero times.)
- 2—Pretty good (I was reminded to be on task two or three times.)
- 1—So-so (I was reminded to be on task more than three times.)

Times of the Day	Target Behavior	
	Student	Staff

Today, I earned _____ points.

_____ points or more = A temporary incentive that the student wants to obtain

Parent signature: _____

Figure 4.8: Example of a CI/CO form.

*Visit **go.SolutionTree.com/RTI** for a free reproducible version of this figure.*

Interventions and Monitoring Within Tier 3

Educators must also be prepared to help students with significant behavioral needs. These students require interventions and monitoring at Tier 3. Tier 3 supports are designed to catch students up when their behavioral skills are far behind their classmates. Tier 2 supports, for both academics and behaviors, are different; they are designed to *prevent* students from falling behind. Tier 2 supports relate directly to the Tier 1 academic priorities that school teams have defined. Tier 3 supports meet the students wherever they may be—and they may have needs with very foundational behavioral skills.

This section will first discuss the impact of precognitive self-regulation deficits on Tier 3 interventions before introducing a research-based approach for determining the causes of a student's significant misbehaviors, as well as the foundational behavioral skills with which the students will require intensive supports: the functional behavioral analysis.

The Impact of Precognitive Self-Regulation Deficits

We frequently find that students needing Tier 3 intervention have deficits in one or more of the domains of precognitive self-regulation that Stuart Shanker (2012), distinguished research professor emeritus of philosophy and psychology at York University, defines in his five domains of self-regulation. The five domains may represent the foundational needs that are inhibiting the success of our most vulnerable students.

1. **The biological:** Attaining, maintaining, regulating, and changing one's level of arousal appropriately for a task or situation, which health, nutrition, sleep, exercise, sensory inputs, and one's ability to process inputs all impact

2. **The emotional:** Controlling, modulating, monitoring, and modifying one's emotions and emotional responses

3. **The cognitive:** Formulating a goal for a task, monitoring goal progress, and adjusting one's behaviors while sustaining and switching attention and responding appropriately; sequencing thoughts, inhibiting impulses, and dealing with frustrations, delays, and distractions

4. **The social:** Managing social interactions, coregulating with others in an empathetic manner, and developing prosocial skills

5. **The educational:** Having awareness of one's academic strengths and weaknesses, with a repertoire of strategies to tackle day-to-day challenges of academic tasks and robust reflective thinking skills (Bronfenbrenner, 1994; Shanker, 2012; Vohs & Baumeister, 2011)

As we explore how to design and implement Tier 3 supports for students, let's revisit a few of the goals identified throughout *Behavior: The Forgotten Curriculum; An RTI Approach for Nurturing Essential Life Skills.*

- Teaching teachers how to read, reframe, and redefine misbehaviors
- Assuming that every student has the capacity to change
- Teaching, modeling, and nurturing appropriate behaviors as a preventative endeavor
- Reframing misbehaviors as stress behaviors
- Helping students recognize stressors
- Ameliorating causes of high stress: within schools and in collaboration with community partners, in neighborhoods, and in homes
- Guiding students to master the steps involved in self-awareness

When the cause of a student's behavioral difficulties stems from an area of precognitive self-regulation, the symptoms will be disruptive to a student's learning and recognizable to educators. Challenges that students may experience as a result of sensitivities to sensory inputs (such as sights and sounds) may show up as difficulties processing or producing language. Environments that challenge a student's abilities to adapt or regulate their emotions or physical movement within may present themselves as ADHD. Examining the *roots of the roots* of difficulties can allow educators to equip students with the strategies to cope and thrive.

Sensations and emotions can overwhelm students unless students develop the capacity to understand and express themselves. Instead of repressing anger, we should teach students to understand, process, and appropriately express anger. Instead of inhibiting, we must become better at teaching students to manage and to regulate. It's not about controlling classrooms or controlling students. It's not about inhibiting negative emotions, exhibiting willpower, or exercising discipline. The better a student can stay calmly focused and alert, the better he gathers, integrates, assimilates, and sequences diverse information for different senses (Shanker, 2012). A calm, focused, and alert student simply has a higher learning capacity. Self-regulation serves as a lens for understanding a student (Shanker, 2012), and for students to understand themselves.

How does this fit inside a daily classroom environment? It starts with having the right mindset—valuing and recognizing the critical importance of these foundational skills. Educators must accept responsibility for helping students develop these skills and believe in their ability to transform lives. They must learn the elements of self-regulation and intentionally prepare for the predictable needs of students. An example of such intentional preparation is classroom and furniture setups that provide options beyond traditional desks and chairs. Tables of various heights, seats of various types, more natural lighting, reductions of background noises (such as from air conditioners), and amplifications of teacher voices are increasingly part of a classroom and school's design and upgrades (Barrett, Davies, Zhang, & Barrett, 2017; Carter, Sebach, & White, 2016). The challenge for educators, and the promise of comprehensive systems of behavioral supports, is identifying the precognitive stressors that lead to cognitive stressors, which may be observed as academic or behavioral difficulties. Too often, discussions of students with significant behavioral needs end in blame or feelings of hopelessness. Instead, let's strive to identify and address the roots of the roots.

The more successes a student experiences with self-regulation, the better he or she can rise to the challenge of mastering ever more complex skills and concepts (Shanker, 2010). One process for developing a positive, proactive, and targeted support for helping a student experience success with self-regulation is a *functional behavioral analysis*.

A Simpler Functional Behavioral Analysis

Functional behavioral analysis "provides staffs with diagnostic information to serve students with more intensive behavioral needs" (Weber, 2015a). It informs the creation of behavior support plans that provide the structures, supports, and reinforcements to help students succeed. It is a collaborative process. Stakeholders who know the student best and, ideally, a behavior specialist (such as school psychologist) should work together to conduct the analysis. Figure 4.9 (page 122) illustrates the process of functional behavioral analysis.

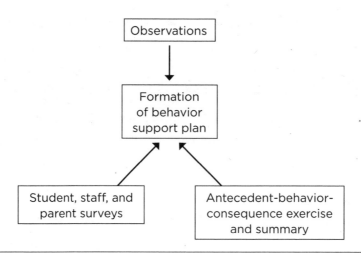

Figure 4.9: Functional behavioral analysis process.

Educators complete a functional behavioral analysis not to find out what's "wrong" with a student, to apply a label, or to confirm a biased preconception, but to determine the positive, wraparound set of supports that will lead to a student's success—supports that they will make concrete in the form of a behavior support plan. The in-depth process of the functional behavioral analysis reveals considerable information about the characteristics and needs of our most vulnerable students, information that subsequently helps educators develop a plan to efficiently serve and support students to success.

The elements and forms comprising a functional behavioral analysis (contained in appendix A) and a behavior support plan (contained in appendix B) are lengthy and extensive, and completing a full functional behavioral analysis will take time. We hope that educators will remain enthusiastic and encouraged to use this method, because the analysis is worth it. Of course, students are worth it, and the students for whom educators complete a functional behavioral analysis are our most vulnerable. We must not give in. We must do whatever we can, expect that our supports will work, and believe in all students' abilities to grow. These processes work best when all team members implement them with consistency, fidelity, patience, and compassion, expecting that all students will achieve success.

Yes, a functional behavioral analysis can be a daunting process with language and steps that some believe only expert psychologists can interpret. That is why we created a functional behavioral analysis from scratch, with input from school psychologists from across the continent, for everyday educators. Please work with your local agencies to ensure that the functional behavioral analysis and behavior support plan align with local requirements.

This functional behavioral analysis (appendix A) includes the following elements.

- **Observation form (Observation Form for Functional Behavioral Analysis, page 140):** A member of the RTI team should complete several observations, for sufficient periods of time, and at different times of the day.

- **Student interviews (Student Interview Form, Student Self-Analysis to Inform Antecedents and Functions of Misbehavior, and Student Self-Reflection Form to Consider Routine, pages 141–147), teacher interviews (Teacher Interview Form and Teacher Analysis to Inform Antecedents and Functions of Misbehavior, pages 148–152), and parent interviews**

(Parent Interview Form and Parent Interview Form to Consider Routine, pages 153–159):
The educator tasked with leading the completion of the functional behavioral analysis should meet with each stakeholder to complete these steps. This step yields far greater information when these interviews occur; we do not recommend that these forms be distributed to each individual to complete independently.

- **Summary form (Summary Form for Functional Behavioral Analysis, pages 160–163):**
A team of relevant educators (the principal, other administrators, special education staff, general education representatives, and a psychologist) should synthesize and analyze any information it gathers to provide each member expertise for the purpose of developing the wraparound plan.

We then provide a template for the behavior support plan (appendix B, page 165), which the information the functional behavioral analysis gathers will inform.

The functional behavioral analysis and behavior support plan are to flow narratively and logically, so we encourage you to read the figures in the appendices as though they were narrative text as you implement them. All figures are also available online in reproducible form at **go.SolutionTree.com/RTI**.

Given the business of educators and the unfamiliarity of behavioral tools for many classroom teachers, we recommend that a member of the schoolwide RTI team (most likely an administrator or special educator) takes the lead on this FBA process. Here's how that would work: the RTI team member would complete observations of the student in various environments across the school—within different classrooms, during different subject areas, at different times, and outside of classrooms (for example, during passing periods and lunch). This team member would then "interview" the teachers with whom the student works, the student's parents, and the student him- or herself. In my experience, "interviewing" individuals has proven to be more efficient and productive than asking staff and parents to complete the forms on their own. The total time required for an RTI team member to complete observations and interviews will vary, but in my experience, it averages ten hours. When these hours are spread across a number of days, the process can be completed in 1½ weeks. The last step, the collaborative completion of the Summary Form, can then be completed by a broader collection of RTI team members.

In my experiences as a school administrator, a few students with significant behavioral needs can consume a very high percentage of time. Contributing to this frustration is that I too often felt that I did not understand the factors that contributed to misbehaviors, and I lacked a plan to help both students and staff succeed. The processes described in this chapter and the details provided in the appendices can inform and empower staff with the skills and tools they require to meet all students' needs.

Restorative Practices at All Three Tiers

Restorative principles and practices apply at all tiers of support and should teach, model, and nurture the behavioral skills that staff and students prioritize. In fact, several high schools in which we have worked conduct restorative justice circles weekly within one of their class periods. These "circles" are secondary school versions of classroom meetings, providing an opportunity for students to come together in a more teen-appropriate way to learn about and discuss behavioral skills and address situations that may have occurred in a positive, collaborative, and problem-solving manner. This reflects restorative practices at Tier 1.

Restorative practices perhaps most meaningfully apply at Tiers 2 and 3. Suspensions do not work (American Psychological Association Zero Tolerance Task Force, 2008; Ball, 2003; Calhoun, 2013; Dupper, Theriot, & Craun, 2009; Gumz & Grant, 2009; Hemphill, Plenty, Herrenkohl, Toumbourou, & Catalano, 2014; Karp & Breslin, 2001; Latimer, Dowden, & Muise, 2005; Mullet, 2014; Skiba, 2014; Tacker & Hoover, 2011; Teasley, 2014; Varnham, 2005). And if staff determine that a suspension is necessary, then they must consider providing Tier 3 supports. Tier 3 supports, as we will describe in the next chapter, involve wraparound supports for students with the most intensive behavioral needs, supports that involve restorative practices. So, what exactly are restorative practices?

Restorative practices flip the script on how we as educators approach misbehaviors. They are not about punishment; they're about reteaching. They are not about educators solving students' problems; they're about students taking responsibility. Restorative practices empower students to resolve conflicts through educator-facilitated, often peer-mediated sessions during which reflection, reteaching, and restitution are the focus. Ryan Jackson, executive principal of the Mount Pleasant Arts Innovation Zone, believes that:

> Schools that adopt a restorative justice mindset and implement those practices truly begin to model empathy and self-discipline, with these skills transferring to students. In my humble opinion, restorative practices have been the most significant development in the area of behavior due to the specific focus on empathy-based teaching and learning as well as their scaffolding of the goal-setting and commitment process for *all* students. The simple reality is that *progress equals happiness,* and the more we can help students identify and celebrate their progress, the better shot we have at students experiencing joy while in school. (R. Jackson, personal communication, June 19, 2017)

Importantly, restorative practices are proactive, action-oriented, and based on social learning. Students in need come together, they make amends, they demonstrate their understanding of how to react and respond in a more productive way, and they return to core learning environments as quickly as possible, and more quickly than they have traditionally.

Strategies within restorative justice include community conferencing, community service, peer juries, conflict mediation, and preventative programs. Here are short summaries of each of these strategies.

- **Community conferencing:** Face-to-face meetings during which the individual (the responsible party) who has negatively impacted an individual or group hears directly from that individual or group (the impacted, affected, or supporting party) regarding how they were affected and how they feel. Those impacted typically have the chance to provide input on restitution—how the situation will be made right, or at least better— and how the entire community will move forward positively. The individual who caused the negative situation also has the opportunity to address the situation.

- **Community service:** A component of restitution may be community service, when the responsible party provides a service to a group within the broader school community. For example, a student responsible for bullying classmates may learn about the negative impacts of bullying and teach minilessons to younger students on how to notice and respond to bullying that they experience or observe.

- **Peer juries:** Peer juries are not courts in which fellow students pass judgment. Students who serve in peer juries work with responsible parties and the impacted, affected, or supporting parties to help repair harm and build skills. Peer juries help support relatively minor situations and are typically guided by a staff member.

- **Conflict mediation:** Also known as peer mediation or conflict resolution, conflict mediation is a structured problem-solving process in which two student facilitators help guide a problem-solving dialogue with two students who have had a conflict (Johnson & Johnson, 1996).

- **Preventative programs:** When patterns of misbehavior occur, schools use the preceding strategies described to provide guidance to a broader group of stakeholders in an effort to prevent future incidents. A common example is bullying prevention; when evidence shows that bullying is becoming a common occurrence, restorative justice circles will address the topic, often with responsible and impacted parties from previous incidents serving as facilitators.

As noted earlier, the principles and practices of restorative justice should be increasingly present within our schools. We believe that they are a fundamental element of Tier 3.

Conclusion

We don't provide interventions so that we can say that we have provided interventions; to check a box or to be compliant; to justify a student's expulsion or justify assessing for special education. We provide interventions because we know that they will work, and we'll do whatever it takes to make that happen.

Core instruction is the most significant and potentially impactful component of a system of supports; Tier 1 is the most important tier. But for a student with supplemental needs, Tier 1, while absolutely necessary, will not be sufficient. Schools must be proactively and systematically prepared with tiered interventions. We hope that this chapter has provided the processes, practices, and tools to support schools as they further develop their RTI-based systems of support that nurture all students' behavioral skills.

Next Steps

The following are next steps for implementing behavioral supports for Tiers 2 and 3.

- Dedicate collaborative time for teams, with support from the schoolwide RTI team, to analyze evidence of student need so that students for whom Tier 2 supports are necessary receive the targeted supports.

- Establish an efficient process for providing Tier 2 supports, with check-in/check-out (CI/CO) serving as the progress-monitoring process. Recruit staff members who can serve as mentors, provide them with ideas and supports, and secure times during which mentors and students can meet.

- With the schoolwide RTI team's guidance, collaborate with school psychologists to learn about functional behavioral analyses and behavior support plans. Determine how to serve more students with significant needs with these tools and how school psychologists can guide other staff in slightly simplified versions of these powerful tools—empowering staff to empower students to behavioral success.

Navigating the
Predictable
Challenges and
Considerations
for Implementation

One child, one teacher, one book, and one pen can change the world. Education is the only solution. Education first.

— MALALA YOUSAFZAI

This final chapter has two interrelated goals: (1) to help educators anticipate common obstacles to successfully implementing behavioral RTI and (2) to suggest ways of patiently persisting through these obstacles, based on our experiences with schools and districts. The chapter will discuss challenges stemming from:

- School culture
- Administrative support
- Schoolwide implementation
- Parents
- Time, staff, and resources
- Data collection, management, and analysis
- Beliefs and expectations
- The need to teach all students

By the end of this chapter, readers should be able to successfully allocate time within the day and resources necessary to guide the work of behavioral RTI, despite any challenges or objections from staff. Leaders should convey their full support for a focus on student behaviors and the expectation that all staff devote time and supports to address all students' behavioral needs.

School Culture

Without a staff culture that recognizes the importance of teaching behavioral skills and displays a commitment to doing so, behavioral RTI will be impossible. Thus, you must acknowledge, respect, and nurture building such a culture from the beginning of your journey. What are the challenges related to culture and designing and implementing a system of behavioral supports for all students, and how can we proactively prepare for them and address them as they arise?

Culture begins at the board and superintendent levels. Leadership empowers and expects site principals to live, breathe, and message the vision that behaviors are as critical as academics, that they model and teach behaviors, and that they realize positive approaches are the best. RTI and educational consultant Jim Wright says:

> Superintendents, district administrators, and building leaders must all understand and support this change. Districts that are successful in promoting positive behaviors among students and staff have established clear, unambiguous, and unwavering support for the goal of positive behaviors across all levels and stakeholders. They create a common language and structure to implement positive behavior management in all buildings, and to collect formative data to evaluate the effectiveness of their efforts. In any building in the district, the principal is tasked with leading the positive-behavior initiative and delivers that message personally, regularly, and consistently in his or her interactions with staff. (J. Wright, personal communication, May 23, 2017)

Long after structures, systems, and processes are in place, culture will determine the extent of a school's sustained success or the frustration of a school's abandonment of what could and should have been successful supports for students.

One way, therefore, that the challenges associated with culture can be addressed is to ensure that behavioral RTI is a priority at the superintendent and board levels, throughout the district office staff, at the site administration level, for the teachers' association, and throughout every classroom. Behavioral RTI will be seen as a priority when leaders communicate a message of its importance consistently and when alignment exists among the various elements of school districts: board priorities and policies, fiscal allocation, personnel allocation, and professional learning initiatives.

Educators were not prepared in our teacher-preparation courses, in most cases, to teach behavioral skills; their training focused on the teaching and learning of academic skills. But the educators honored to serve students, families, and communities can learn, and there is as much research and as many research-based practices in the area of motivation as there are in the content area of mathematics (Deci, 1992; Dweck et al., 2014; Pintrich & Schunk, 2002; Ryan & Deci, 2000; Stipek, 1988; Wentzel, 1997; Yair, 2000; Zimmerman et al., 1992). Our schools must embrace a culture that

> help[s] students move from being passive recipients of academic content to active learners who can manage their workload, assess their progress and status, persist in difficult tasks, and develop a reliable set of strategies to master increasingly complex academic content as they proceed through school. (Farrington et al., 2012, p. 5)

Other ways to address the challenges of building buy-in for the shifts associated with behavioral RTI are to:

- Share the statistics that we provided in the introduction of this book (page 1)

- Have staff take the survey that we provide in chapter 1 (page 18)

- Engage in honest, positive conversations around current staff realities and attitudes, and the needs of communities and students

Lastly, change of any kind is challenging, and change and culture are related. Change can be intimidating and even resisted, in my experience, when stakeholders experience the following.

- They don't understand the purpose and need for the change. Therefore, communicate the *why*, using the information within the introduction (page 1).

- They don't have the training or resources to feel and be successful throughout the change. Drawing on the information within this book, make a commitment to providing the time, resources, and professional learning supports that staff need and deserve.

- They don't see how the change benefits them and those they serve. Therefore, gather and communicate evidence on the progress and successes occurring as a result of the change, either directly or indirectly. For example, if the behavioral skills described in the book improve, tardies should decrease, attendance should increase, D and F grades should decrease, work completion should increase, and behavioral infractions should decrease, to name five data points that schools already regularly gather.

- They aren't held accountable to make the change. Therefore, check in frequently, provide opportunities for collaboration to occur, and patiently but persistently hold all staff accountable for the changes upon which consensus was reached.

- They are unaware of a clear process. This book, I hope, provides a comprehensive plan to follow when initiating and implementing the changes that are required when committing to improving students' behavioral skills.

Administrative Support

Leadership is critical in all school functions that intend to significantly improve student outcomes. Administrators listen, learn, serve, and support. In the area of schoolwide behaviors, administrative support is especially critical.

Behavioral expectations and processes are schoolwide; while grade-level teams, departmental teams, and collaborative teams may have success on their own, only a schoolwide team is best positioned to guide this endeavor. Of course, teacher representatives are part of the schoolwide teams that lead behavior, but administrators, who have a schoolwide focus, should take the lead. Moreover, we want grade-level teams, departmental teams, and collaborative teams to focus on teaching and learning within their grade levels and content areas; in these areas, they take the lead. While all staff members assume collective responsibility for nurturing behavioral skills, administrators serve as the content-area experts.

To meet this challenge, behavioral RTI and systems of support should be led by the leadership team under the direct guidance of the school principal (Buffum et al., 2012). While all staff members are involved and responsible for ensuring the success of behavioral RTI, the school's leadership must take the lead on coordinating efforts.

Last, when helping staff help students develop positive behavioral skills, timely and focused follow-through is critical. Administrators are in the best position to systematically and proactively accomplish these tasks, getting out of the office, into classrooms, and being present. Stated another way (and at the risk of oversimplifying), teacher teams take the lead on academic skills and concepts, and administrators take the lead on behavioral skills and concepts (even though all staff members collaborate on both).

So, have a plan that prioritizes administrators' active and timely support of behaviors, particularly when students exhibit behaviors that interrupt learning environments, using processes such as those described in chapter 3 (page 59).

Schoolwide Implementation

Consistency is vital to helping students successfully develop positive and productive behavioral skills, and consistency requires a schoolwide, systematic approach to teaching. What does this mean? Well, while different grade levels and departments will likely have unique priorities for academic skills and concepts, behavioral expectations, routines, procedures, and processes must be the same among staff members, classrooms, and environments to achieve optimal success.

The obvious challenge to this is that students increasingly spend significant amounts of time with multiple educators and staff members throughout the day. We set both students and fellow staff up for frustration when rules and procedures are different depending on where and with whom a student happens to be. Sure, horizontal and vertical articulation and consistencies are important when planning and preparing for academic teaching and learning; but mindsets, social skills, perseverance, learning strategies, and academic behaviors can be and probably should be the same across classrooms, courses, and grade levels. As Farrington and colleagues (2012) note:

> A students' sense of belonging, self-efficacy, and interest will be shaped by their experiences in the classroom, their interactions with the teacher and fellow classmates, their prevailing beliefs about their own ability, and the nature of the work they are asked to do. (p. 74)

Establishing and maintaining consistencies for what teachers do to reinforce behaviors, and for what students' behavioral success looks and sounds like across the school campus, are fundamental.

Parents

We're often asked, "What is the parents' role in response to intervention, in behavioral supports, and in education?" Our response is typically, "What have you told them their role is?" Parents can be incredible partners in our joint effort to ensure that all students are future ready, but we can and must take the lead on defining what expectations should be and how families can complement the primary efforts of schools.

To meet these challenges, share homework policies, grading policies, and information about next-generation standards with parents, and also share with parents the *why*, *how*, and *what* of schools' expectations and supports in the areas of mindsets, social skills, perseverance, learning strategies, and academic behaviors. Specify how parents can reinforce these skills in the home. Explain why these skills are more important than ever and describe what it takes to be successful in college and a skilled career. We should not expect parents to already possess this knowledge, and we cannot expect them to impart these sophisticated and critical behavioral skills to their children—at least not without our support. Again, *we* are the answer we've been waiting for.

And, take steps to empower parents to succeed and to strengthen the school-home partnership. Some strategies can include involving parents early, engaging them in a determination of the skills that the broader community most wants students to possess (see chapter 1, page 15). Also, involve parents in the measuring of student progress in these behavioral skills (see chapter 3, page 59). And teach parents about the unwritten rules of schools (including the importance of noncognitive factors) and how they can support their children in developing the skills that help them navigate these rules.

Time, Staff, and Resources

Perhaps the most common frustration that we hear from educators is an absence of resources—enough time to provide supports, enough staff to provide supports, the appropriate strategies and programs, and the money for all of it. We hope that we've provided options for the use of time and staff, and suggestions for research-based strategies and programs within this book, but before reviewing, we feel compelled to quote Ronald Edmonds (1979), the father of the Effective Schools movement:

> It seems to me, therefore, that what is left of this discussion are three declarative statements: (a) We can, whenever and wherever we choose, successfully teach all children whose schooling is of interest to us; (b) We already know more than we need to do that; and (c) Whether or not we do it must finally depend on how we feel about the fact that we haven't so far. (p. 23)

The time to teach, model, and nurture can and must be built into school days, and educators can and must integrate behavioral skills into the teaching and learning of academic concepts and skills. (See Finding Time for Instruction in chapter 2, page 48, for strategies.)

In terms of workable strategies, while all staff must be involved in the consistent, collaborative modeling and teaching of behavioral skills, administrators and psychologists can take an even greater lead in supporting staff in the aid of students. There need not be (and most likely will not be) additional staff hired to teach behaviors—we're all teaching behaviors whether we like it and know it or not (Buffum et al., 2009, 2010, 2012). Researched-based strategies and programs exist, and we've provided targeted suggestions in chapters 3 (page 59) and 4 (page 93), but the best strategies are a fierce commitment to nurturing behavioral skills and building strong positive relationships.

Last, while more financial resources would be welcome, repurposing time and staff does not cost money, and there are free or low-cost resources available for supporting behavioral skills. A favorite resource of districts and schools in which I work and have worked is Jim Wright's Intervention Central source for RTI resources (Wright, n.d.). Other schools are effectively and efficiently leveraging the time and staff that we currently have. The research exists. The resources exist. Educators have the skill; it's up to us to decide if we also have the will.

Data Collection, Management, and Analysis

We urge educators to prioritize the use of assessments and evidence to inform practices in both behavior and academics. The assessment of noncognitive factors is an emerging field, and while observations and surveys may have reliability and validity complications, educators can use tools such as those provided in chapter 3 (page 61) to capture evidence to inform *who* needs *what* in a timely manner.

Gathering accurate data represents a challenge. Managing data efficiently represents a challenge. Using the data productively and in a timely manner represents a challenge. In addition to the tools provided at the beginning of chapter 3 (page 61), which provide schools with tools for gathering data in efficient ways that provide accurate information, there are also ways of managing this information and using it to inform future teaching and learning. The steps described in chapter 4 (page 93) can help staff manage data. Software solutions also exist that will facilitate the management of evidence of behavioral skills. Two software solutions that may decrease the time required to gather behavioral data and to manage and use behavioral data are Intervention Compass (www.interventioncompass.com) and Kickboard (www.kickboardforschools.com). Both programs help staff share data information, stay connected when supporting students, and monitor the success of students.

Regarding processes for the impactful use of data, we recommend, as we have throughout the book, that schools follow the same protocols that they use to analyze data related to academic concepts and skills. Data-analysis guides exist (see chapter 3, figures 4.1 and 4.2, page 100 and 101), teams already regularly devote time to reviewing and responding to academic data, and professional learning communities and data teams already prescribe steps to guide educators. School leadership teams and teacher teams can thus successfully transfer data analysis skills and processes from academics to behaviors.

Beliefs and Expectations

Beyond a collaborative culture, a belief in the ability of all students to learn (academic and behavioral skills) at high levels is fundamental. Students know when educators have high expectations for their success (Zimmerman et al., 1992). When educators have high expectations, students learn at higher levels. There can be no references to *that student* or *those students*. No label can be allowed to persuade educators that students cannot self-regulate, be motivated, or be cooperative. With proactive and positive supports, educators can make significant progress, and all students can be on track (or get back on track) for college, career, and future readiness. We have experienced it, and researchers demonstrate that the behavioral skills described throughout this book are malleable (Farrington et al., 2012).

Educators cannot use a perceived lack of student motivation as an excuse to deny supports to students. Motivation is a symptom. More specifically, motivation is an academic behavior (see chapter 1, page 15). A student's needs in the areas of precognitive self-regulation, mindsets, social skills, perseverance, or learning strategies will likely lead to a lack of motivation.

An absence of high expectations is a challenge. How do we overcome this challenge? I recommend that schools develop an action plan that describes concrete steps that will be taken to promote more positive student and staff mindsets such as the following, directly related to the indicators provided by Camille Farrington and her colleagues (2012) and described in the introduction.

- "I belong in this academic community." Some steps that could be taken to increase students' connections to school include (1) initiating or reinvigorating homerooms or advisory periods within secondary schools or classroom meetings in elementary schools; (2) keeping track of interactions within classrooms to ensure that a conversation (however brief) happens with every student at least every week; and (3) expanding the quantity and type of activities or clubs at school so that every student can be involved, connected to something on campus, and held accountable to being involved.

- "My ability and competence grow with my effort." Some steps that could increase student and staff beliefs that, given time and the right supports, all students can learn at a high level are (1) stopping assigning points when work (quizzes, papers, tests) is returned, and starting to highlight errors (opportunities for improvement) that all students are expected to correct or improve; (2) stopping assigning *zeroes* that effectively let students off the hook, instead assigning *incompletes* and requiring students to complete all assignments that were worthy of being assigned in the first place; (3) requiring students to refine assignments and retake tests that are below an agreed-upon level of mastery, instead of denying them the opportunity to show you what they now know after correcting errors, relearning concepts, and receiving support; (4) consistently communicating a "not yet" approach to lack of understanding, as in, "I don't get this yet," instead of "I don't get this"; and (5) explicitly learning from errors, using a routine like "My Favorite No" (www.teachingchannel.org/videos/class-warm-up-routine), in which a "good" mistake is shared with the class as an opportunity to grow.

- "I can succeed at this." Some steps that could increase student and staff beliefs that success with the task is possible include (1) learning about, and truly committing to, differentiation and scaffolding—for example, providing text that is at students' reading level so that they can access science or social studies content, or adjusting the complexity of numbers so that students can be successful accessing mathematics concepts; and (2) providing students with multiple ways of showing what they know—for example, videoing, screencasting, or recording audio of responses.

- "This work has value for me." In addition to striving to design experiences that tap into students' lives, promote more voice, choice, and agency to increase the value that students place on their learning in the following ways. Voice: listen to students and use their input when providing options for the content with which they engage, process used for learning, and products they use to show what they know. Choice: allow students to exercise some choice over the place, pace, path, and time of day that they learn. Agency: give students a stake in their learning, inviting (or requiring) them to track their progress toward learning.

The Need to Teach All Students

Schools implementing behavioral RTI sometimes believe that the teaching, modeling, and nurturing of behavioral skills are only for "naughty" students, students at risk, or students from historically underperforming subgroups. This could not be further from the truth. As we have evidenced throughout this book, all students will benefit from developing more effective behavioral skills. Too often, behavioral RTI (and academic RTI, for that matter) efforts only focus on intervention, or Tiers 2 and 3. Having a Tier 1 focus means that all students receive supports in the behavioral skills needed for success in school, college, career, and life. All means all. We have met high-achieving students who do not persevere, and gifted students with fixed mindsets. Schools need not worry about when they will pull vulnerable students to teach them behavioral skills. The teaching and learning of behavioral skills are for all, and must be part of every school's Tier 1, core environments.

There may be educators who feel that a focus on behavioral skills is now unnecessary, given the increasing popularity of facilitated learning experiences, project-based learning, the maker movement, and competency-based education (Colby, 2017; Dougherty & Conrad, 2016; Larmer, Mergendoller, & Boss, 2015). In other words, perhaps more contemporary pedagogies and practices (present in a growing number of future ready schools) already represent the answer to the question, "How do we nurture behavioral skills within students?" They very well may, but while next-generation teaching may be more facilitative and learning may be more experiential, students still need guidance, to see adults modeling good habits, and to receive behavioral skills instruction. As Farrington and colleagues (2012) report:

> Students are not likely to develop learning strategies in the absence either of explicit instruction or classwork that requires the use of such strategies. It may be most helpful to think about noncognitive factors as properties of the interactions between students and classrooms or school environments. Rather than being helpless in the face of students who lack perseverance and good academic behaviors, teachers set the classroom conditions that strongly shape the nature of students' academic performance. The essential question is not how to change students to improve their behavior but rather how to create contexts that better support students in developing critical attitudes and learning strategies necessary for their academic success. Thus, teaching adolescents to become learners may require educators to shift their own beliefs and practices as well as to build their pedagogical skills and strategies to support student learning in new ways. Academic behaviors and perseverance may need to be thought of as creations of school and classroom contexts rather than as personal qualities that students bring with them to school. (p. 72)

So how do educators do it? What silver bullet or magic formula will help teachers and schools help students develop these habits? While there may be unique strategies about which educators do not know, the practices that are likely to help develop critical behavioral skills are the very same research-based best practices about which educators have read but may not have found time to implement or have not implemented well—rigorous and relevant teaching, collaborative learning, and differentiated instruction, to name a few.

Conclusion

Although challenges may abound when implementing a new curriculum—particularly a curriculum that feels new—the importance of ensuring students develop positive and productive behavioral skills is a moral imperative. We must do whatever it takes to overcome any challenges that arise.

Next Steps

The following are next steps for preparing to overcome challenges in implementing behavioral RTI.

- With your leadership team, begin to define the *why* behind behavioral RTI and to build a case for improving supports for students. Begin to plan for a patient but persistent process for involving more stakeholders in the process and for doing the work described in this book.

- Anticipate challenges that may emerge and develop plans to meet these needs. Reach out to other districts, schools, experts with experiences in behavioral RTI, and those who have experienced difficulties and overcome them.

- Develop a communication plan for when, to whom, and how ongoing efforts to nurture behaviors will be shared with stakeholders and how feedback from stakeholders will be heard and incorporated into ongoing efforts.

Epilogue

The research is clear. We understand the realities. The nature of the futures for which we are preparing students is undeniable. *We*, as educators, are the answer we've been waiting for to help students develop the behavioral skills they need to succeed in school, college, work, and life.

It is my hope that *Behavior: The Forgotten Curriculum; An RTI Approach for Nurturing Essential Life Skills* illustrates the clear need for educators to teach behavioral skills to students with the same emphasis that they place on academics. I have provided strategies and templates for teaching these skills to all students at the Tier 1 level, tips for implementing and monitoring supports at Tiers 2 and 3, and assistance in providing effective feedback and differentiation. I have identified predictable challenges that may occur and listed ways to overcome these. The task is now up to you!

Perhaps most significantly, I have aligned a process for behavioral RTI to the more familiar process of academic RTI with which I and others have had experience and success, from PLC at Work through the three tiers of RTI. In addition, I have encouraged educators' understandings of behavior from beyond social skills to include mindsets, learning strategies, perseverance, and academic behaviors.

I wish you luck as you work with your team, step-by-step, through this book to strive to implement a schoolwide system of behavioral RTI in your schools and districts. The legacy you'll leave your students, families, communities, and society will be profound.

Appendix A:
Functional Behavioral Analysis

The practical Functional Behavioral Analysis (FBA) and the Behavior Support Plan (BSP; appendix B, page 165) are original designs based on exceptional, more formal FBAs and BSPs. See, for example, the FBA and BSP guidance from the Connecticut State Department of Education (http://www.portal.ct.gov/-/media/SDE /Publications/edguide/FunctionalBehavioralAssessmentandModelForm.pdf). We also drew inspiration from Crone, Hawken, & Horner (2015) and Buck, Polloway, Kirkpatrick, Patton, & Fad (2000). We started from scratch in designing an FBA and BSP to ensure that general education teachers, and administrators who are former general education teachers, could use these tools confidently and competently. We attempted to keep jargon out to enable users to link the FBA to the BSP whenever possible.

Observation Form for Functional Behavioral Analysis

Observations

Observation Number	Note the specifics of behavioral incidents that occur.			
	Define and describe the misbehavior. (This will inform step 1 of the summary.)	Describe the outcome, consequence, or reinforcement of the misbehavior. (This will inform step 2 of the summary.)	Describe when and where the misbehavior occurs. (This will inform steps 3a and 3b of the summary.)	Describe with whom and with what the misbehavior occurs. (This will inform steps 3c and 3d of the summary.)
1				
2				
3				
4				
5				
6				
7				
8				

Student Interview Form

Student Interview

To begin, say something like, "We're gathering information in order to better understand what goes on in and out of the classroom. We would like to know your point of view, and we need your help getting an accurate picture of what's going on. Please answer openly and honestly."

Student name: _____   Grade: _____

Interviewer: _____   Date: _____

Interests and Strengths

Ask the student, "What do you like to do, and what do you do well in school and outside of school?" Then, write down what the student says in the following spaces.

- In school: _____
- Outside of school: _____

Misbehaviors

Use the questions in the following chart to focus on when, where, with whom, and with what misbehaviors occur.

Can you specifically describe the challenges that occur?	What happens after you react to those challenges?	When do challenges seem to occur?	What are you doing or what are you asked to do when challenges occur?	How often does this happen? (Direct the student to rate him- or herself on a scale of 1 to 4, where 1 means *rarely* and 4 means *a lot.*)	How likely do you think it is that this will happen again? (Direct the student to rate him- or herself on a scale of 1 to 4, where 1 means *rarely* and 4 means *a lot.*)
Step 1	Step 2	Steps 3a and 3b	Steps 3c and 3d		

Behavior: The Forgotten Curriculum; An RTI Approach for Nurturing Essential Life Skills © 2018 Solution Tree Press
SolutionTree.com • Visit **go.SolutionTree.com/RTI** to download this free reproducible.

Use the questions in the following chart to focus on what challenges, misbehaviors, or both, the student ranks highest.

What are the challenges or misbehaviors? (step 1)	What were the environments, antecedents, and causes? (step 3)

Use the questions in the following chart to focus on what specific behaviors lead to challenges.

Questions	Notes
Do you think that what goes on outside of school affects how a student works and behaves in class? How?	
What about you? What is happening in your life outside of school that affects you while you're in school?	
Most students are bothered by someone or something that goes on at school. Who or what bothers you?	

To complete the following chart, present the student with a copy of this table and ask him or her to rank (from 1 to 9) the specific events that they believe most led to their frustrations or challenges. Then record their rankings in the table.

_____ Arriving late; tardy	_____ Pushing, shoving, hitting, fighting	_____ Bullying or threatening people
_____ Not seeming to care	_____ Using bad language or mean language	_____ Disrupting class
_____ Destroying materials	_____ Destroying property	_____ Missing class; absent

Answer the following questions to conclude.

• Describe what you feel *before* you get in trouble.

• Describe what you do when you get in trouble.

• Share how long the challenge, problem, or trouble usually lasts.

• Describe what you feel *after* you get in trouble.

Student Self-Analysis Form

Choose one misbehavior or challenge on which to focus: _____

Use the following chart to determine which statement(s) seems to describe what's happening when the misbehavior or challenge occurs.

Statement	Follow-Up Questions
☐ I'm not sure what to do.	
☐ There's nothing to do.	
☐ My classmates are bugging me.	
☐ I'm sitting by a certain classmate.	
☐ I'm working alone.	
☐ The teacher keeps telling me what to do.	
☐ I'm having a bad day.	
☐ The teacher keeps telling me what not to do.	
☐ The work is too hard.	
☐ The work is too easy.	
☐ The work is too boring or too long.	
☐ The work is too long.	
☐ I need to talk to the teacher.	
☐ I need help.	

Student Self-Analysis to Inform Antecedents and Functions of Misbehavior

Use the following chart to answer why you sometimes act out.

Statement	Follow-Up Questions
☐ To get adults to pay attention to me or talk to me	
☐ To get classmates to pay attention to me, look at me, talk to me, or laugh at me	
☐ To get to do something that I want to do	
☐ To get things that I want	
☐ To avoid doing things that are too hard	
☐ To avoid things that I don't like	
☐ So I'm not bored	
☐ Because things are too easy	
☐ To avoid working with classmates I don't like	
☐ To avoid adults I don't like	
☐ Because I don't like people telling me what to do	

Student Self-Reflection Form to Consider Routine

Self-Analysis of Routine

Use the following chart to reflect on your routines.

How would you describe your routines?	On a scale of 1 to 4, how many routines do you have? (1 means *not a lot of routines*; 4 means *a lot of routines*.)

Use the following chart to determine what types of things get in the way of having helpful routines.

Things That Get in the Way	Follow-Up Questions
☐ Hunger	
☐ Lack of sleep	
☐ Trouble at home	
☐ Trouble at school	
☐ Homework not done	
☐ Missed medication	
☐ Illness; feeling sick	
☐ Confusion; don't understand the subject	

Behavior: The Forgotten Curriculum; An RTI Approach for Nurturing Essential Life Skills © 2018 Solution Tree Press
SolutionTree.com • Visit **go.SolutionTree.com/RTI** to download this free reproducible.

Use the questions in the following chart to wrap up your reflections.

Closing Questions	Notes
Can you think of any times or situations in school that you would avoid if you could?	
In what classes or situations do you feel most successful?	
In what classes or situations is your behavior the best?	
Can you think of anything that you wish would happen that doesn't happen often or at all?	
Can you name one or two things you wish were different about school?	
Can you name one or two things you wish were different outside of school?	
Can you name one or two things you wish were different about yourself?	

Teacher Interview Form

Teacher Interview

When using this form to interview teachers, begin by saying something like, "We're gathering information in order to better understand what goes on for this student in your classroom. We would like to know your point of view, and we need your help getting an accurate picture of what's going on. Please answer openly and honestly."

Student name: _____ Grade: _____

Teacher name: _____ Course or subject with student: _____

Interviewer: _____ Date: _____

Interests and Strengths

Describe your student's strengths in and outside of school.

- In school: _____
- Outside of school: _____

Misbehaviors

Use the questions in the following chart to focus on when, where, with whom, and with what misbehaviors occur.

Can you specifically describe the misbehaviors that occur?	What consequences are given when these misbehaviors occur?	When do misbehaviors seem to occur?	What is the student doing or asked to do when misbehaviors occur?	How often have you observed these misbehaviors occurring?	How likely do you think it is that the student will display this misbehavior again?
Step 1	Step 2	Steps 3a and 3b	Steps 3c and 3d		

Use the following chart to focus on which misbehaviors the student ranks highest.

What are the challenges or misbehaviors? (Step 1)	What were the environments, antecedents, and causes? (Step 3)

Before analysis:

- Describe any behaviors you notice before misbehaviors occur.

- State how long the incidents last.

Teacher Analysis to Inform Antecedents and Functions of Misbehavior

Choose one misbehavior on which to focus: _____

Ask yourself, "Which of the following statements seem to describe what's happening when the student misbehaves?"

Statement	Follow-Up Questions
☐ The student does not seem to understand directions.	
☐ The task is less structured.	
☐ Classmates are irritating the student.	
☐ The student is irritating classmates.	
☐ The student is sitting near a certain classmate.	
☐ The student is working alone.	
☐ The student is working with classmates.	
☐ It's during small-group instruction.	
☐ It's during whole-group instruction.	
☐ It's during transitions.	
☐ The task seems too hard.	
☐ The task seems too easy.	

page 1 of 3

Behavior: The Forgotten Curriculum; An RTI Approach for Nurturing Essential Life Skills © 2018 Solution Tree Press
SolutionTree.com • Visit **go.SolutionTree.com/RTI** to download this free reproducible.

Statement	Follow-Up Questions
☐ The task seems too long.	
☐ The task is physically demanding.	
☐ The student has been corrected.	
☐ The student has been reprimanded.	

Use the following chart to focus on why the student seems to misbehave. Ask yourself, "Why is this student misbehaving?"

Statement	Follow-Up Questions
☐ For adult attention	
☐ For peer attention	
☐ For access to a preferred activity or task	
☐ To avoid an activity or task	
☐ To acquire objects	
☐ For sensory stimulation	
☐ To avoid sensory stimulation	
☐ To avoid interactions with others	

Use the following chart to focus on what types of things seem to exacerbate situations or lead to misbehavior.

Factors That Exacerbate Misbehavior or Get in the Way	Follow-Up Questions
☐ Hunger	
☐ Lack of sleep	
☐ Trouble at home	
☐ Trouble at school	
☐ Homework not done	
☐ Missed medication	
☐ Illness; feeling sick	
☐ Confusion; doesn't understand the subject	

Consider the following closing questions and jot down any notes about them.

Closing Questions	Notes
What classes, people, or situations does the student try to avoid?	
What people or situations *should* the student try to avoid?	
In what classes or situations do you feel that the student is most successful?	
In what classes or situations is the student's behavior the best?	

Parent Interview Form

Parent Interview

When using this form to interview parents, begin by saying something like, "We're gathering information in order to better understand what goes on in and out of the classroom for your child. We would like to know your point of view, and we need your help getting an accurate picture of what's going on. Please answer openly and honestly."

Student name: _____ Grade: _____

Parent name: _____

Interviewer: _____ Date: _____

Interests and Strengths

Ask parents or guardians, "What does your child like to do, and what do they do well in and outside of school?" Record their responses.

- In school: _____

- Outside of school: _____

Misbehaviors

Use the questions in the following chart to focus on when, where, with whom, and with what the misbehaviors occur.

Can you specifically describe the challenges that occur?	How does your child react when this occurs?	When do challenges seem to occur for your child?	What is your child doing or asked to do when challenges occur?	How often does this happen? (Use a scale of 1 to 4 with 1 meaning *rarely* and 4 meaning *a lot*.)	How likely do you think it is that this will happen again? (Use a scale of 1 to 4 with 1 meaning *rarely* and 4 meaning *a lot*.)
Step 1	Step 2	Steps 3a and 3b	Steps 3c and 3d		

Use the following chart to determine what challenges or misbehaviors the parent ranked highest.

What are the challenges or misbehaviors? (step 1)	What were the environments, antecedents, and causes? (step 3)

Use the following opening questions to focus on what specific behaviors lead to challenges.

Opening Questions	Notes
Do you think that what goes on outside of school affects how your child works and behaves in class? How?	
What's unique about your child? What is happening in your child's life outside of school that affects them while in school?	
Most students are bothered by someone or something that goes on at school. Who or what bothers your child?	

Use the following chart to identify and then rank with parents the specific behaviors that parents believe lead to their child's challenges.

____ Arriving late; tardy	____ Pushing, shoving, hitting, fighting	____ Bullying or threatening people
____ Not seeming to care	____ Bad language or mean language	____ Disrupting class
____ Destroying materials	____ Destroying property	____ Missing class; absent

Compile the parents' answers to conclude.

- Describe what you believe your child feels *before* getting in trouble.

Behavior: The Forgotten Curriculum; An RTI Approach for Nurturing Essential Life Skills © 2018 Solution Tree Press
SolutionTree.com • Visit **go.SolutionTree.com/RTI** to download this free reproducible.

- Describe how you believe your child behaves when he or she gets in trouble.

- State how long you believe your child's behavior usually lasts.

- State how often this seems to happen.

- Describe how you think your child responds *after* getting in trouble.

Behavior: The Forgotten Curriculum; An RTI Approach for Nurturing Essential Life Skills © 2018 Solution Tree Press
SolutionTree.com • Visit **go.SolutionTree.com/RTI** to download this free reproducible.

Parent Interview Form to Consider Routine

Parental Analysis to Inform Antecedents (what comes before the misbehavior) and Functions (the purpose of the misbehavior)

Using the following chart, choose one misbehavior on which to focus: _____

Ask parents, "Which of the following statements seem to describe what's happening when your child misbehaves?"

Statement	Follow-Up Questions
☐ My child does not seem to understand directions.	
☐ The task is less structured.	
☐ Classmates are irritating my child.	
☐ My child is irritating classmates.	
☐ My child is sitting near a certain classmate.	
☐ My child is working alone.	
☐ My child is working with classmates.	
☐ It's during small-group instruction.	
☐ It's during whole-group instruction.	
☐ It's during transitions.	
☐ The task seems too hard.	

☐ The task seems too easy.	
☐ The task seems too long.	
☐ The task is physically demanding.	
☐ My child has been corrected.	
☐ My child has been reprimanded.	

Use the following chart to determine why a parent thinks his or her child seems to misbehave.

Statement	Follow-Up Questions
☐ For adult attention	
☐ For peer attention	
☐ For access to a preferred activity or task	
☐ To avoid an activity or task	
☐ To acquire objects	
☐ For sensory stimulation	
☐ To avoid sensory stimulation	
☐ To avoid interactions with others	

Use the following chart to determine what routines the parent has in place for his or her child.

How would you describe your child's routines?	On a scale of 1 to 4, with 1 meaning *not a lot of routines* and 4 meaning *a lot of routines*, how many routines would you say your child has?

Use the following chart to determine what types of things get in the way of having helpful routines.

Things That Get in the Way	Follow-Up Questions
☐ Hunger	
☐ Lack of sleep	
☐ Trouble at home	
☐ Trouble at school	
☐ Homework not done	
☐ Missed medication	
☐ Illness; feeling sick	
☐ Confusion; doesn't understand the subject	

Closing

Use the following questions to conclude the conference.

Closing Questions	Notes
Can you think of any times or situations in school that your child would really avoid if possible?	
In what classes or situations does your child feel most successful?	
In what classes or situations is your child's behavior the best?	
Can you think of anything that you wish would happen that doesn't happen often or at all for your child?	
Can you name one or two things you wish were different about school for your child?	
Can you name one or two things you wish were different outside of school for your child?	

Behavior: The Forgotten Curriculum; An RTI Approach for Nurturing Essential Life Skills © 2018 Solution Tree Press
SolutionTree.com • Visit **go.SolutionTree.com/RTI** to download this free reproducible.

Summary Form for Functional Behavioral Analysis

Three-Step Summary:

1. Examine the observation forms' notes and identify patterns and trends.

2. Examine the interview forms' notes and responses and identify patterns and trends.

3. Complete the following steps.

Step 1: Define and describe the misbehavior.	Step 2: State the consequence or reinforcement the student receives due to his or her misbehavior.	Step 3: Define behaviors and the environment that immediately precede the misbehavior.	Step 4: State what the student seems to be seeking.

Step 1: Define and Describe the Misbehavior

Key Questions to Consider	Notes
What do the teacher or staff observe?	
What can the teacher or staff measure?	
What can the teacher or staff describe?	
What words do the student and staff use?	
What actions do the student or staff take?	

Step 2: State the Consequence or Reinforcement the Student Receives Due to His or Her Misbehavior

Key Questions to Consider	Notes
What consequence do the teacher or staff assign as a result of the misbehavior?	
How soon after the misbehavior do the teacher or staff assign the consequence?	
What is the student's reaction to the consequence?	

Step 3: Define Behaviors and the Environment That Immediately Precede the Misbehavior

When, Where, With Whom, With What, and Under What Conditions Is the Misbehavior Occurring?		Notes
When	What time of day	
	After a break or immediately after another class period or subject area	
	During whole-group instruction	
	During small-group instruction	
	During less structured times—breaks, recesses, lunch	
Where	In class—the front, the back	
	Out of class—hallways, playground, cafeteria	
With whom	Same gender	
	Opposite gender	
	Working independently	
	Working with peers	
	Specific individuals	
With what	Reading	
	Writing	
	Mathematics	
	Multistep or longer-term tasks	
	Assessments	
	More open-ended or more ambiguously defined tasks	
Under what conditions	Appears tired	
	Appears hungry	
	Appears distracted	
	Appears troubled	
	Triggers seem to prompt or exacerbate	
	Other behaviors that seem to immediately precede	
Describe situations that result in more positive behaviors.	When	
	Where	
	With whom	
	With what	
	Under what conditions	

Step 4: State What the Student Seems to Be Seeking

Why Is the Misbehavior Occurring?	What Is the Student Specifically Seeking?	Notes
To obtain	Peer attention	
	Adult attention	
	Desired activity	
	Desired objects or items	
	Desired response	
	Sensory stimulation (tactile, auditory, visual)	
	Social interaction	
To avoid	Difficult task	
	Boring task	
	Easy task	
	Physical demands	
	Non-preferred activity	
	Peer	
	Adults	
	Reprimand	

Consider the following questions:

- Does the student's behavior significantly differ from that of his or her classmates?

- Does the behavior lessen the possibility of successful learning for the student or others?

- Have past efforts to address the behavior using standard interventions been unsuccessful?

- Does the behavior represent a skill or performance deficit, rather than a cultural difference?

- Are there significant or mild academic deficits that may be contributing to behavioral difficulties?

- Is the behavior serious, persistent, chronic, or a threat to the safety of the student or others?

Categorize behavior—Is the misbehavior linked to a skill deficit or a performance deficit?

- **Skill deficit:** A behavioral or academic skill that the student does not know how to perform. Example: In a disagreement, the student hits the other student because he does not know other strategies for conflict resolution. In cases of skill deficit, the behavior support plan needs to describe how the skill will be taught and how the student will be supported while learning it.

- **Performance deficit:** A behavioral or academic skill the student does know, but does not consistently perform. Example: A student is chronically late for the classes she doesn't "like." In cases of performance deficit, the behavior support plan may include strategies to increase motivation.

Form a hypothesis to inform the behavior support plan.

Conditions (Record when, where, with whom, and with what.)	Student Response (Predict the misbehavior.)	Reason (Determine the purpose or function.)

Appendix B:
Behavior Support Plan

Behavior Support Plan

Target

Identify the target misbehaviors, desired behaviors, and goal from functional behavioral analysis.

Clearly define and describe the **misbehavior.**	Clearly define and describe the desired **behavior.**	Specifically define the frequency and duration at which the student will display the desired behavior to achieve success.

Preventative Supports

Match redirection, prevention, and de-escalation strategies and replacement behaviors.

Describe how the student and staff will **redirect** misbehaviors *when they begin* to occur or *after they begin* to occur.	Describe **precorrections** that staff will provide and preventative supports that staff will employ before the misbehavior is *likely to occur.*	Describe the **de-escalation strategies** that student and staff will use when the misbehavior *begins to occur.*	Describe a **replacement behavior** that meets the identified function and that staff agree is temporarily acceptable *instead of* the misbehavior.

Follow-Up

Explicitly describe the staff member's responses when misbehaviors occur.

Behavior or Misbehavior*	**Actions** when the misbehavior occurs**	**Feedback** that staff will provide when the behavior or misbehavior occurs	**Positive reinforcement** that staff will provide when the desired behavior occurs	**Progress monitoring** of the plan's success***

*Use the misbehavior from the preceding table.

**Use if / then to explain. For example, "If [misbehavior] occurs, then [specific action] will occur with [specific staff member] or with [other staff member] if the first individual is unavailable."

***Use CI/CO template, page 119. The same CI/CO process used to monitor student progress at Tier 2 can be used within the BSP. Consider checking in and out more frequently throughout the day. In this column, specify when and with whom progress on each target behavior will be monitored.

Five steps to follow when misbehaviors occur:

1. Acknowledge the misbehavior.
2. Describe who has been affected and how (adults, peers, oneself).
3. Determine the needs of those the misbehavior affects.
4. Explain how to make restitution (apologies, service, or something else).
5. Figure out what reteaching to provide.

Acknowledgement of misbehavior	Affected parties (Include adults, peers, oneself.)	Needs of those the misbehavior affects	Possible restitution	Reteaching that needs to occur

Four restorative justice steps to complete when misbehaviors occur:

1. Determine what processes or products the student can complete to demonstrate understanding and to make restitution.
2. Determine how and when a successful return to the environment will occur.
3. Consider using restorative practice strategies, described in chapter 4 (such as peer juries and conflict mediation).
4. Specify follow-up date or dates.

Processes or products the student can use to **demonstrate understanding** and to **make restitution**	How and when a successful **return** to the environment will occur	Which **restorative practice strategies** will be used	Follow-up dates

Interventions

Use the following to plan Tier 3 support within small groups or for individuals.

Program	Target Behavior or Misbehavior	Ensure Initial and Ongoing Professional Development*	When, Where, for How Long, and With Whom**	Progress Monitor Using CI/CO Procedures***
Aggression Replacement Training (www.aggression replacementtraining.com)	Physical respect and aggression			
Cognitive Behavioral Intervention for Trauma in Schools (CBITS; https://cbitsprogram.org)	Childhood trauma			
FIRST STEP Next (https://pacificnwpublish.com/products/FIRST-STEP-Next.html)	Prosocial skill development			
The Incredible Years (www.incredibleyears.com)	Social and emotional competencies			
Check & Connect (http://checkandconnect.umn.edu)	Engagement, motivation, apathy			
Anger Coping	Anger management			

*School leaders should ensure that educators facilitating these supports receive appropriate and sufficient professional learning supports. Specify the types and dates here.

**State when, where, for how long, and with whom the student will receive support.

***The same CI/CO process used to monitor student progress at Tier 2 can be used within the BSP. Consider checking in and out more frequently throughout the day. In this column, specify when and with whom progress on the behavior that the program is targeting will be monitored.

Brief Descriptions of Tier 3 Behavioral Programs

Aggression Replacement Training	A research-based approach with three components: 1. **Social skills training**—Helping students replace antisocial behaviors with positive alternatives 2. **Anger control training**—Helping students respond to anger in a nonaggressive manner and rethink anger-provoking situations 3. **Moral reasoning training**—Helping enhance students' level of fairness, justice, and concern for the needs and rights of others
CBITS	CBITS helps reduce symptoms of post-traumatic stress disorder (PTSD), depression, and behavioral problems, and to improve functioning, grades and attendance, peer and parent support, and coping skills.
FIRST STEP Next	FIRST STEP Next teaches skills that contribute to school success and the development of friendships. It's ideal for students who exhibit challenging behaviors such as defiance, conflicts with peers, and disruptive behaviors.
The Incredible Years	This preschool and early elementary program strengthens young children's social and emotional competencies, such as understanding and communicating feelings, using effective problem-solving strategies, managing anger, practicing friendship and conversational skills, and behaving appropriately in the classroom.
Check & Connect	This program supports high school students in making life choices that enhance their chances of graduating, communicates strong messages about the importance of persisting in school, teaches effective problem-solving strategies and conflict-resolution skills, helps develop a plan for making responsible life choices, helps find productive extracurricular activities during the school year and summer, and encourages parents to stay actively involved.
Anger Coping	Anger Coping focuses on developing anger-management skills through group intervention sessions that aim to improve perspective taking, problem-solving skills, recognition of emotions associated with anger arousal, and strategies for managing conflicts.

Professional Development

Use the following chart to describe how and when to provide professional development. Each staff member involved with implementing the plan deserves and requires professional learning supports to successfully serve the student.

Which staff and stakeholders require training?	In what specific areas do staff require training?	With what strategies or programs do the staff require training?	When will the school (or district) provide initial and ongoing training?

References and Resources

ACT. (2012). *The condition of college and career readiness.* Iowa City, IA: Author.

Ainsworth, L. (2010). *Rigorous curriculum design: How to create curricular units of study that align standards, instruction, and assessment.* Englewood, CO: Lead + Learn Press.

Allen, J., Gregory, A., Mikami, A., Lun, J., Hamre, B., & Pianta, R. (2013). Observations of effective teacher-student interactions in secondary school classrooms: Predicting student achievement with the Classroom Assessment Scoring System—Secondary. *School Psychology Review, 42*(1), 76–98.

Allington, R. L. (2011). What at-risk readers need. *Educational Leadership, 68*(6), 40–45.

American Psychological Association Zero Tolerance Task Force. (2008). Are zero tolerance policies effective in the schools? *American Psychologist, 63*(9), 852–862.

Baker, J. A. (2006). Contributions of teacher-child relationships to positive school adjustment during elementary school. *Journal of School Psychology, 44*(3), 211–229.

Ball, R. (2003). Restorative justice as strength-based accountability. *Reclaiming Children and Youth: The Journal of Strength-based Interventions, 12*(1), 49–52.

Bangert-Drowns, R. L., Kulik, C.-L. C., Kulik, J. A., & Morgan, M. T. (1991). The instructional effect of feedback in test-like events. *Review of Educational Research, 61*(2), 213–238.

Barrett, P., Davies, F., Zhang, Y., & Barrett, L. (2017). The holistic impact of classroom spaces on learning in specific subjects. *Environment and Behavior, 49*(4), 425–451.

Battistich, V., Schaps, E., & Wilson, N. (2004). Effects of an elementary school intervention on students' "connectedness" to school and social adjustment during middle school. *Journal of Primary Prevention, 24*(3), 243–262.

Benson, J. (2012). 100 repetitions. *Educational Leadership, 70*(2), 76–78.

Berry, D., & O'Connor, E. (2009). Behavioral risk, teacher-child relationships, and social skill development across middle childhood: A child-by-environment analysis of change. *Journal of Applied Developmental Psychology, 31*(1), 1–14.

Blair, C., & Diamond, A. (2008). Biological processes in prevention and intervention: The promotion of self-regulation as a means of preventing school failure. *Development and Psychopathology, 20*(3), 899–911.

Bloom, B. S. (1968). Learning for mastery. *Evaluation Comment, 1*(2), 1–12.

Bloom, B. S. (1974). Time and learning. *American Psychologist, 29*(9), 682–688.

Bloom, B. S. (1984). The search for methods of group instruction as effective as one-to-one tutoring. *Educational Leadership, 41*(8), 4–17.

Borghans, L., Golsteyn, B. H. H., Heckman, J. J., & Humphries, J. E. (2016). *What grades and achievement tests measure*. Bonn, Germany: Institute for the Study of Labor.

Boynton, M., & Boynton, C. (2005). *The educator's guide to preventing and solving discipline problems*. Alexandria, VA: Association for Supervision and Curriculum Development.

Braithwaite, R. (2001). *Managing aggression*. New York: Routledge.

Brock, S. E. (1998). Helping the student with ADHD in the classroom: Strategies for teachers. *Communiqué, 26*(5), 18–20.

Bronfenbrenner, U. (1994). Ecological models of human development. In T. Husen & T. N. Postlethwaite (Eds.), *International encyclopedia of education* (2nd ed., Vol. 3, pp. 1643–1647). Oxford, England: Pergamon Press.

Buck, G. H., Polloway, E. A., Kirkpatrick, M. A., Patton, J. R., and Fad, K.M. (2000). Developing behavioral intervention plans: A sequential approach. *Intervention in School and Clinic, 36*(1), 3–9.

Buffum, A., Mattos, M., & Weber, C. (2009). *Pyramid response to intervention: RTI, professional learning communities, and how to respond when kids don't learn*. Bloomington, IN: Solution Tree Press.

Buffum, A., Mattos, M., & Weber, C. (2010). The why behind RTI. *Educational Leadership, 68*(2), 10–16.

Buffum, A., Mattos, M., & Weber, C. (2012). *Simplifying response to intervention: Four essential guiding principles*. Bloomington, IN: Solution Tree Press.

Buffum, A., Mattos, M., Weber, C., & Hierck, T. (2015). *Uniting academic and behavior interventions: Solving the skill or will dilemma*. Bloomington, IN: Solution Tree Press.

Burns, M. K., Appleton, J. J., & Stehouwer, J. D. (2005). Meta-analysis of response-to-intervention research: Examining field-based and research-implemented models. *Journal of Psychoeducational Assessment, 23*(4), 381–394.

Burns, M. K., & Symington, T. (2002). A meta-analysis of prereferral intervention teams: Student and systemic outcomes. *Journal of School Psychology, 40*(5), 437–447.

Calhoun, A. (2013). Introducing restorative justice: Re-visioning responses to wrongdoing. *Prevention Researcher, 20*(1), 3–6.

Campbell, A., & Anderson, C. M. (2011). Check-in/check-out: A systematic evaluation and component analysis. *Journal of Applied Behavioral Analysis, 44*(2), 315–326.

Carnine, D. W. (1976). Effects of two teacher-presentation rates on off-task behavior, answering correctly, and participation. *Journal of Applied Behavior Analysis, 9*(2), 199–206.

Carr, E. G., Dunlap, G., Horner, R. H., Koegel, R. L., Turnbull, A. P., Sailor, W., et al. (2002). Positive behavior support: Evolution of an applied science. *Journal of Positive Behavior Interventions, 4*(1), 4–16.

Carter, D., Sebach, G., & White, M. (2016). *What's in your space: 5 steps for better classroom and school design*. Thousand Oaks, CA: Corwin Press.

Center for Responsive Schools. (2015). *The first six weeks of school: From Responsive Classroom*. Turners Falls, MA: Author.

Cheema, J. R., & Kitsantas, A. (2014). Influences of disciplinary classroom climate on high school student self-efficacy and mathematics achievement: A look at gender and racial–ethnic differences. *International Journal of Science and Mathematics Education, 12*(5), 1261–1279.

Colby, R. L. (2017). *Competency-based education: A new architecture for K–12 schooling*. Cambridge, MA: Harvard Education Press.

Collaborative for Academic, Social, and Emotional Learning. (2018). *Assessment work group: Establishing practical social-emotional competence assessments of preschool to high school students.* Accessed at https://casel.org/assessment-work-group on February 3, 2018.

Colvin, G., Sugai, G., Good, R. H., III, & Lee, Y.-Y. (1997). Using active supervision and pre-correction to improve transition behaviors in an elementary school. *School Psychology Quarterly, 12*(4), 344–363.

Conley, D. T. (2014). *Getting ready for college, careers, and the Common Core.* San Francisco: Jossey-Bass.

Cook, C. R., Rasetshwane, K. B., Truelson, E., Grant, S., Dart, E. H., Collins, T. A., et al. (2011). Development and validation of the Student Internalizing Behavior Screener: Examination of reliability, validity, and classification accuracy. *Assessment for Effective Intervention, 36*(2), 71–79.

Covey, S. (2014). *The 7 habits of highly effective teens: Personal workbook.* New York: Touchstone.

Crone, D. A., Hawken, L. S., & Horner, R. H. (2015). *Building positive behavior support systems in schools: Functional behavior assessment* (2nd ed.). New York: Guilford Press.

Curwin, R. (2015, August 11). *13 common sayings to avoid* [Blog post]. Accessed at www.edutopia.org/blog/13-common-sayings-to-avoid-richard-curwin on October 3, 2017.

Curwin, R. L., & Mendler, A. N. (1999). *Discipline with dignity.* Alexandria, VA: Association for Supervision and Curriculum Development.

Deci, E. L. (1992). The relation of interest to the motivation of behavior: A self-determination theory perspective. In K. A. Renninger, S. Hidi, & A. Krapp (Eds.), *The role of interest in learning and development* (pp. 43–71). Hillsdale, NJ: Erlbaum.

Deming, D. J. (2015). *The growing importance of social skills in the labor market* (NBER Working Paper No. 21473). Cambridge, MA: National Bureau of Economic Research.

Denton, P. (2005). *Learning through academic choice.* Turners Falls, MA: Center for Responsive Schools.

DeNavas-Walt, C., & Proctor, B. D. (2014, September). *Income and poverty in the United States: 2013.* Washington, DC: U.S. Census Bureau. Accessed at www.census.gov/content/dam/census/library/publications/2014/demo/p60-249.pdf on October 3, 2017.

De Pry, R. L., & Sugai, G. (2002). The effect of active supervision and pre-correction on minor behavioral incidents in a sixth grade general education classroom. *Journal of Behavioral Education, 11*(4), 255–267.

Dougherty, D., & Conrad, A. (2016). *Free to make: How the maker movement is changing our schools, our jobs, and our minds.* Berkeley, CA: North Atlantic Books.

Drummond, T. (1994). *The Student Risk Screening Scale (SRSS).* Grants Pass, OR: Josephine County Mental Health Program.

Duckworth, A. L. (2016). *Grit: The power of passion and perseverance.* New York: Scribner.

Duckworth, A. L., & Carlson, S. M. (2013). Self-regulation and school success. In B. W. Sokol, F. M. E. Grouzet, & U. Müller (Eds.), *Self-regulation and autonomy: Social and developmental dimensions of human conduct* (pp. 208–230). New York: Cambridge University Press.

Duckworth, A. L., Quinn, P. D., & Tsukayama, E. (2012). What No Child Left Behind leaves behind: The roles of IQ and self-control in predicting standardized achievement test scores and report card grades. *Journal of Educational Psychology, 104*(2), 439–451.

Duckworth, A. L., & Seligman, M. E. P. (2005). Self-discipline outdoes IQ in predicting academic performance of adolescents. *Psychological Science, 16*(12), 939–944.

DuFour, R., DuFour, R., Eaker, R., Many, T., & Mattos, M. (2010). *Learning by doing: A handbook for Professional Learning Communities at Work* (2nd ed.). Bloomington, IN: Solution Tree Press.

DuFour, R., DuFour, R., Eaker, R., Many, T., & Mattos, M. (2016). *Learning by doing: A handbook for Professional Learning Communities at Work* (3rd ed.). Bloomington, IN: Solution Tree Press.

DuPaul, G. J., & Ervin, R. A. (1996). Functional assessment of behaviors related to attention-deficit/hyperactivity disorder: Linking assessment to intervention design. *Behavior Therapy, 27*(4), 601–622.

DuPaul, G. J., & Stoner, G. (2003). *ADHD in the schools: Assessment and intervention strategies* (2nd ed.). New York: Guilford Press.

Dupper, D. R., Theriot, M. T., & Craun, S. W. (2009). Reducing out-of-school suspensions: Practice guidelines for school social workers. *Children and Schools, 31*(1), 6–14.

Dweck, C. S. (2006). *Mindset: The new psychology of success.* New York: Random House.

Dweck, C. S., Walton, G. M., & Cohen, G. L. (2014). *Academic tenacity: Mindsets and skills that promote long-term learning.* Seattle, WA: Bill & Melinda Gates Foundation.

Edmonds, R. (1979). Effective schools for the urban poor. *Educational Leadership, 37*(1), 15–18, 20–24.

Elbaum, B., Vaughn, S., Hughes, M., & Moody, S. (2000). How effective are one-to-one tutoring programs in reading for elementary students at risk for reading failure? A meta-analysis of the intervention research. *Journal of Educational Psychology, 92*(4), 605–619.

Elswick, S. (2018). *Using picture books to enhance children's social and emotional literacy: Creative activities and programs for parents and professionals.* London: Kingsley.

Ennis, C. E. (1996). When avoiding confrontation leads to avoiding content: Disruptive students' impact on curriculum. *Journal of Curriculum and Supervision, 11*(2), 145–162.

Ericsson, K. A., & Pool, R. (2016). *Peak: Secrets from the new science of expertise.* Boston: Houghton Mifflin Harcourt.

Farrington, C. A., Roderick, M., Allensworth, E., Nagaoka, J., Keyes, T. S., Johnson, D. W., et al. (2012). *Teaching adolescents to become learners: The role of noncognitive factors in shaping school performance—A critical literature review.* Chicago: University of Chicago Consortium on Chicago School Research.

Forbes, H. T. (2012). *Help for Billy: A beyond consequences approach to helping challenging children in the classroom.* Boulder, CO: Beyond Consequences Institute.

Ford, A. D., Olmi, D. J., Edwards, R. P., & Tingstrom, D. H. (2001). The sequential introduction of compliance training components with elementary-aged children in general education classroom settings. *School Psychology Quarterly, 16*(2), 142–157.

Gabe, T. (2015). *Poverty in the United States: 2013.* Washington, DC: Congressional Research Service.

Gersten, R., Beckmann, S., Clarke, B., Foegen, A., Marsh, L., Star, J. R., et al. (2009). *Assisting students struggling with mathematics: Response to intervention for elementary and middle schools.* Washington, DC: National Center for Education Evaluation and Regional Assistance.

Gersten, R., Compton, D., Connor, C. M., Dimino, J., Santoro, L., Linan-Thompson, S., et al. (2008). *Assisting students struggling with reading: Response to intervention (RtI) and multi-tier intervention in the primary grades.* Washington, DC: National Center for Education Evaluation and Regional Assistance.

Gettinger, M. (1988). Methods of proactive classroom management. *School Psychology Review, 17*(2), 227–242.

Gettinger, M., & Seibert, J. K. (2002). Best practices in increasing academic learning time. In A. Thomas (Ed.), *Best practices in school psychology* (4th ed., Vol. 1, pp. 773–787). Bethesda, MD: National Association of School Psychologists.

Gregory, A., Cornell, D., Fan, X., Sheras, P., Shih, T.-H., & Huang, F. (2010). Authoritative school discipline: High school practices associated with lower bullying and victimization. *Journal of Educational Psychology, 102*(2), 483–496.

Gumz, E. J., & Grant, C. L. (2009). Restorative justice: A systematic review of the social work literature. *Families in Society, 90*(1), 119–126.

Guskey, T. R. (2010). Lessons of mastery learning. *Educational Leadership, 68*(2), 52–57.

Hardin, C. J. (2008). *Effective classroom management: Models and strategies for today's classrooms* (2nd ed.). Upper Saddle River, NJ: Pearson.

Hattie, J. (2009). *Visible learning: A synthesis of over 800 meta-analyses relating to achievement.* New York: Routledge.

Hattie, J. (2012). *Visible learning for teachers: Maximizing impact on learning.* New York: Routledge.

Hattie, J., Biggs, J., & Purdie, N. (1996). Effects of learning skills interventions on student learning: A meta-analysis. *Review of Educational Research, 66*(2), 99–136.

Hattie, J., & Timperley, H. (2007). The power of feedback. *Review of Educational Research, 77*(1), 81–112.

Hattie, J., & Yates, G. C. R. (2014). *Visible learning and the science of how we learn.* New York: Routledge.

Hawken, L. S., & Horner, R. H. (2003). Evaluation of a targeted intervention within a schoolwide system of behavior support. *Journal of Behavioral Education, 12*(3), 225–240.

Haydon, T., & Scott, T. M. (2008). Using common sense in common settings: Active supervision and precorrection in the morning gym. *Intervention in School and Clinic, 43*(5), 283–290.

Heckman, J. J., & Kautz, T. (2012). Hard evidence on soft skills. *Labour Economics, 19*(4), 451–464.

Hemphill, S. A., Plenty, S. M., Herrenkohl, T. I., Toumbourou, J. W., & Catalano, R. F. (2014). Student and school factors associated with school suspension: A multilevel analysis of students in Victoria, Australia and Washington State, United States. *Children and Youth Services Review, 36*(1), 187–194.

Heward, W. L. (1994). Three "low-tech" strategies for increasing the frequency of active student response during group instruction. In R. Gardner III, D. M. Sainato, J. O. Cooper, T. E. Heron, W. L. Heward, J. Eshleman, et al. (Eds.), *Behavior analysis in education: Focus on measurably superior instruction* (pp. 283–320). Monterey, CA: Brooks/Cole.

Hierck, T., Coleman, C., & Weber, C. (2011). *Pyramid of behavior interventions: Seven keys to a positive learning environment.* Bloomington, IN: Solution Tree Press.

Hoffmann, K., Cooper, G., & Powell, B. (2017). *Raising a secure child: How circle of security parenting can help you nurture your child's attachment, emotional resilience, and freedom to explore.* New York: The Guilford Press.

Hughes, J. N., Cavell, T. A., & Willson, V. (2001). Further support for the developmental significance of the quality of the teacher-student relationship. *Journal of School Psychology, 39*(4), 289–301.

Jacobs, G. M., Power, M. A., & Inn, L. W. (2002). *The teacher's sourcebook for cooperative learning: Practical techniques, basic principles, and frequently asked questions.* Thousand Oaks, CA: Corwin Press.

Jacobs, H. H. (1997). *Mapping the big picture: Integrating curriculum and assessment K–12.* Alexandria, VA: Association for Supervision and Curriculum Development.

Jacobs, H. H. (2004). *Getting results with curriculum mapping.* Alexandria, VA: Association for Supervision and Curriculum Development.

Johnson, D. W., & Johnson, R. T. (1996). Conflict resolution and peer mediation programs in elementary and secondary schools: A review of the research. *Review of Educational Research, 66*(4), 459–506.

Johnson, D. W., Johnson, R. T., & Holubec, E. J. (2013). *Cooperation in the classroom* (8th ed.). Edina, MN: Interaction Book.

Karp, D. R., & Breslin, B. (2001). Restorative justice in school communities. *Youth and Society, 33*(2), 249–272.

Klem, A. M., & Connell, J. P. (2004). Relationships matter: Linking teacher support to student engagement and achievement. *Journal of School Health, 74*(7), 262–273.

Kluger, A. N., & DeNisi, A. (1996). The effects of feedback interventions on performance: A historical review, a meta-analysis, and a preliminary feedback intervention theory. *Psychological Bulletin, 119*(2), 254–284.

Kohn, A. (1992). *No contest: The case against competition* (Rev. ed.). Boston, MA: Houghton Mifflin.

Lampi, A. R., Fenty, N. S., & Beaunae, C. (2005). Making the three Ps easier: Praise, proximity, and precorrection. *Beyond Behavior, 15*(1), 8–12.

Lanceley, F. J. (1999). *On-scene guide for crisis negotiators.* Boca Raton, FL: CRC Press.

Lane, K. L., Bruhn, A. L., Eisner, S. L., & Kalberg, J. R. (2010). Score reliability and validity of the Student Risk Screening Scale: A psychometrically sound, feasible tool for use in urban middle schools. *Journal of Emotional and Behavioral Disorders, 18*(4), 211–224.

Lane, K. L, Kalberg, J. R., Lambert, W. E., Crnobori, M., & Bruhn, A. L. (2010). A comparison of systematic screening tools for emotional and behavioral disorders: A replication. *Journal of Emotional and Behavioral Disorders, 18*(2), 100–112.

Lane, K. L., Kalberg, J. R., Parks, R. J., & Carter, E. W. (2008). Student Risk Screening Scale: Initial evidence for score reliability and validity at the high school level. *Journal of Emotional and Behavioral Disorders, 16*(3), 178–190.

Lane, K. L., Little, M. A., Casey, A. M., Lambert, W., Wehby, J., Weisenbach, J. L., et al. (2009). A comparison of systematic screening tools for emotional and behavioral disorders: How do they compare? *Journal of Emotional and Behavioral Disorders, 17*(2), 93–105.

Lane, K. L., Menzies, H. M., Bruhn, A. L., & Crnobori, M. (2011). *Managing challenging behaviors in schools: Research-based strategies that work.* New York: Guilford Press.

Lane, K. L., Oakes, W. P., Ennis, R. P., Cox, M. L., Schatschneider, C., & Lambert, W. (2011). Additional evidence for the reliability and validity of the Student Risk Screening Scale at the high school level: A replication and extension. *Journal of Emotional and Behavioral Disorders, 21*(2), 97–115.

Lane, K. L., Parks, R. J., Kalberg, J. R., & Carter, E. W. (2007). Systematic screening at the middle school level: Score reliability and validity of the Student Risk Screening Scale. *Journal of Emotional and Behavioral Disorders, 15*(4), 209–222.

Lansbury, J. (2014). *No bad kids: Toddler discipline without shame.* Los Angeles: JLML Press.

Larmer, J., Mergendoller, J., & Boss. S. (2015). *Setting the standard for project-based learning: A proven approach to rigorous classroom instruction.* Alexandria, VA: Association for Supervision and Curriculum Development.

Larson, M. R., & Kanold, T. D. (2016). *Balancing the equation: A guide to school mathematics for educators and parents.* Bloomington, IN: Solution Tree Press.

Latimer, J., Dowden, C., & Muise, D. (2005). The effectiveness of restorative justice practices: A meta-analysis. *The Prison Journal, 85*(2), 127–144.

Lewis, T. J., Colvin, G., & Sugai, G. (2000). The effects of pre-correction and active supervision on the recess behavior of elementary students. *Education and Treatment of Children, 23*(2), 109–121.

Liew, J., Chen, Q., & Hughes, J. N. (2010). Child effortful control, teacher-student relationships, and achievement in academically at-risk children: Additive and interactive effects. *Early Childhood Research Quarterly, 25*(1), 51–64.

Long, N. J., Morse, W. C., & Newman, R. G. (Eds.) (1980). *Conflict in the classroom: The education of emotionally disturbed children* (4th ed.). Belmont, CA: Wadsworth.

Martens, B. K., Hiralall, A. S., & Bradley, T. A. (1997). A note to teacher: Improving student behavior through goal setting and feedback. *School Psychology Quarterly, 12*(1), 33–41.

Martens, B. K., & Kelly, S. Q. (1993). A behavioral analysis of effective teaching. *School Psychology Quarterly, 8*(1), 10–26.

Martens, B. K., & Meller, P. J. (1990). The application of behavioral principles to educational settings. In T. B. Gutkin & C. R. Reynolds (Eds.), *The handbook of school psychology* (2nd ed., pp. 612–634). New York: Wiley.

Marzano, R. J. (2003). *What works in schools: Translating research into action.* Alexandria, VA: Association for Supervision and Curriculum Development.

Marzano, R. J., Pickering, D. J., & Pollock, J. E. (2001). *Classroom instruction that works: Research-based strategies for increasing student achievement.* Alexandria, VA: Association for Supervision and Curriculum Development.

Maslow, A. H. (1943). A theory of human motivation. *Psychological Review, 50(4)*, 370–396.

Maslow, A. H. (1954). *Motivation and personality.* New York: Harper & Row.

Masten, A. S., & Coatsworth, J. D. (1998). The development of competence in favorable and unfavorable environments: Lessons from research on successful children. *American Psychologist, 53*(2), 205–220.

Mayer, G. R. (2000). *Classroom management: A California resource guide.* Los Angeles: County Office of Education. Accessed at https://minisink.com/fileadmin/user_upload/es/ClassroomManagement.pdf on April 9, 2018.

Mayer, G. R., & Ybarra, W. J. (2003). *Teaching alternative behaviors schoolwide: A resource guide to prevent discipline problems.* Los Angeles: County Office of Education. Accessed at www.worldcat.org/title/teaching-alternative-behaviors-schoolwide-a-resource-guide-to-prevent-discipline-problems/oclc/317962652 on April 9, 2018.

McKeon, D. (2005). *Research talking points on English language learners.* New York: National Education Association.

Menzies, H. M., & Lane, K. L. (2012). Validity of the Student Risk Screening Scale: Evidence of predictive validity in a diverse, suburban elementary setting. *Journal of Emotional and Behavioral Disorders, 20*(2), 82–91.

Miao, Y., Darch, C., & Rabren, K. (2002). Use of precorrection strategies to enhance reading performance of students with learning and behavior problems. *Journal of Instructional Psychology, 29*(3), 162–174.

Milan, F. B., Parish, S. J., & Reichgott, M. J. (2006). A model for educational feedback based on clinical communication skills strategies: Beyond the "feedback sandwich." *Teaching and Learning in Medicine, 18(1)*, 42–47.

Mischel, W. (2014). *The marshmallow test: Mastering self-control.* New York: Little, Brown.

Mouzakitis, A., Codding, R. S., & Tryon, G. (2015). The effects of self-monitoring and performance feedback on the treatment integrity of behavior intervention plan implementation and generalization. *Journal of Positive Behavior Interventions, 17*(4), 223–234.

Mullet, J. H. (2014). Restorative discipline: From getting even to getting well. *Children and Schools, 36*(3), 157–162.

National Governors Association Center for Best Practices & Council of Chief State School Officers. (2010). *Common Core State Standards for English language arts and literacy in history/social studies, science, and technical subjects.* Washington, DC: Authors. Accessed at www.corestandards.org/assets/CCSSI_ELA%20Standards.pdf on January 26, 2018.

No Child Left Behind Act of 2001, Pub. L. No. 107–110, 20 U.S.C. § 6319 (2002).

Noftle, E. E., & Robins, R. W. (2007). Personality predictors of academic outcomes: Big Five correlates of GPA and SAT scores. *Journal of Personality and Social Psychology, 93*(1), 116–130.

Oakes, W. P., Wilder, K. S., Lane, K. L., Powers, L., Yokoyama, L. T. K., O'Hare, M. E., et al. (2010). Psychometric properties of the Student Risk Screening Scale: An effective tool for use in diverse urban elementary schools. *Assessment for Effective Intervention, 35*(4), 231–239.

O'Connor, E., & McCartney, K. (2007). Examining teacher-child relationships and achievement as part of an ecological model of development. *American Educational Research Journal, 44*(2), 340–369.

Partnership for 21st Century Learning. (2016). *Framework for 21st century learning.* Accessed at www.p21.org /storage/documents/docs/P21_framework_0816.pdf on February 3, 2018.

Pfaff, M. E. (2000, April). *The effects on teacher efficacy of school-based collaborative activities structured as professional study groups.* Paper presented at the annual meeting of the American Educational Research Association, New Orleans, LA.

Pintrich, P. R., & Schunk, D. H. (2002). *Motivation in education: Theory, research, and applications* (2nd ed.). Columbus, OH: Merrill Prentice Hall.

Poropat, A. E. (2009). A meta-analysis of the five-factor model of personality and academic performance. *Psychological Bulletin, 135*(2), 322–338.

Powell, S., & Nelson, B. (1997). Effects of choosing academic assignments on a student with attention deficit hyperactivity disorder. *Journal of Applied Behavior Analysis, 30*(1), 181–183.

Reddy, R., Rhodes, J. E., & Mulhall, P. (2003). The influence of teacher support on student adjustment in the middle school years: A latent growth curve study. *Development and Psychopathology, 15*(1), 119–138.

Resmovits, J., & Phillips, A. M. (2017, September 17). Students' progress stalls on California's standardized tests. *Los Angeles Times.* Accessed at www.latimes/local/education/la-me-california-test-scores-20170827-story.html on April 9, 2018.

Ribble, M. (2014). *Digital citizenship defined: Teach the 9 elements to enhance students' safety, creativity and empathy.* Accessed at http://edtech.ospi.k12.wa.us/pluginfile.php/9649/mod_resource/content/0/Digital_Citizenship _ISTE.pdf on April 9, 2018.

Ryan, R. M., & Deci, E. L. (2000). Intrinsic and extrinsic motivations: Classic definitions and new directions. *Contemporary Educational Psychology, 25*(1), 54–67.

Schanzenbach, D. W., Nunn, R., Bauer, L., Mumford, M., & Breitwieser, A. (2016). *Seven facts on noncognitive skills from education to the labor market.* Washington, DC: Brookings Institution.

Scherer, M. (2001). How and why standards can improve student achievement: A conversation with Robert J. Marzano. *Educational Leadership, 59*(1), 14–18.

Schlechty, P. C. (2002). *Working on the work: An action plan for teachers, principals, and superintendents.* San Francisco: Jossey-Bass.

Schmoker, M. (2004). Learning communities at the crossroads: A response to Joyce and Cook. *Phi Delta Kappan*, *86*(1), 84–89.

Seita, J. (2014). Reclaiming disconnected kids. *Reclaiming Children and Youth*, *23*(1), 28–32.

Shanker, S. G. (2012). *Calm, alert, and learning: Classroom strategies for self-regulation*. Toronto, Ontario, Canada: Pearson.

Shute, V. J. (2008). Focus on formative feedback. *Review of Educational Research*, *78*(1), 153–189.

Simonsen, B., Fairbanks, S., Briesch, A., Myers, D., & Sugai, G. (2008). Evidence-based practices in classroom management: Considerations for research to practice. *Education and Treatment of Children*, *31*(3), 351–380.

Skiba, R. J. (2014). The failure of zero tolerance. *Reclaiming Children and Youth*, *22*(4), 27–33.

Skiba, R. J., & Peterson, R. L. (2000). School discipline at a crossroads: For zero tolerance to early response. *Exceptional Children*, *66*(3), 335–347.

Sousa, D. A., & Tomlinson, C. A. (2011). *Differentiation and the brain: How neuroscience supports the learner-friendly classroom*. Bloomington, IN: Solution Tree Press.

Sousa, D. A., & Tomlinson, C. A. (2018). *Differentiation and the brain: How neuroscience supports the learner-friendly classroom* (2nd ed.). Bloomington, IN: Solution Tree Press.

Sprick, R. S., Borgmeier, C., & Nolet, V. (2002). Prevention and management of behavior problems in secondary schools. In M. A. Shinn, H. M. Walker, & G. Stoner (Eds.), *Interventions for academic and behavior problems II: Preventive and remedial approaches* (pp. 373–401). Bethesda, MD: National Association of School Psychologists.

Stiggins, R. (2006). Assessment for learning: A key for motivation and learning. *Phi Delta Kappan*, *2*(2), 3–19.

Stipek, D. J. (1988). *Motivation to learn: From theory to practice*. Englewood Cliffs, NJ: Prentice Hall.

Stormont, M. A., Smith, S. C., & Lewis, T. J. (2007). Teacher implementation of precorrection and praise statements in Head Start classrooms as a component of a program-wide system of positive behavioral support. *Journal of Behavioral Education*, *16*(3), 280–290.

Sugai, G. (2001, June). *School climate and discipline: Schoolwide positive behavior support*. Keynote presentation to and paper for the National Summit on the Shared Implementation of Individuals with Disabilities Education Act, Washington, DC.

Sugai, G., & Horner, R. H. (2002). The evolution of discipline practices: School-wide positive behavior supports. *Child and Family Behavior Therapy*, *24*(1–2), 23–50.

Suitts, S. (2015). *A new majority research bulletin: Low income students now a majority in the nation's public schools*. Atlanta, GA: Southern Education Foundation.

Swanson, H. L., & Sachse-Lee, C. (2000). A meta-analysis of single-subject-design intervention research for students with LD. *Journal of Learning Disabilities*, *33*(2), 114–136.

Tabary, Z. (2015, April 20). *The skills agenda: Preparing students for the future* [Blog post]. Accessed at www .eiuperspectives.economist.com/talent-education/driving-skills-agenda/blog/skills-agenda-preparing-students -future on November 27, 2017.

Tacker, M. K., & Hoover, J. H. (2011). Restorative circles in schools. *Reclaiming Children and Youth*, *20*(1), 59–60.

Teasley, M. L. (2014). Shifting from zero tolerance to restorative justice in schools. *Children and Schools*, *36*(3), 131–133.

TEDx Talks. (2014, November 4). *Ryan Jackson: How competition ignites educational success* [Video file]. Accessed at www.youtube.com/watch?v=7BgpzBnKDIU on November 27, 2017.

Theirworld. (2016). *Malala Yousafzai's speech at the Youth Takeover of the United Nations.* Accessed at https://theirworld.org/explainers/malala-yousafzais-speech-at-the-youth-takeover-of-the-united-nations on April 8, 2018.

Thompson, G. J., & Jenkins, J. B. (1993). *Verbal judo: The gentle art of persuasion.* New York: Morrow.

Todd, A. W., Campbell, A. L., Meyer, G. G., & Horner, R. H. (2008). The effects of a targeted intervention to reduce problem behaviors: Elementary school implementation of check in—check out. *Journal of Positive Behavior Interventions, 10*(1), 46–55.

Tomlinson, C. A. (2014). *The differentiated classroom: Responding to the needs of all learners* (2nd ed.). Alexandria, VA: Association for Supervision and Curriculum Development.

Tough, P. (2012). *How children succeed: Grit, curiosity, and the hidden power of character.* Boston: Houghton Mifflin Harcourt.

Tough, P. (2016). *Helping children succeed: What works and why.* Boston: Houghton Mifflin Harcourt.

Trope, Y., & Neter, E. (1994). Reconciling competing motives in self evaluation: The role of self-control in feedback seeking. *Journal of Personality and Social Psychology, 66*(4), 646–657.

Udelhofen. S. (2014). *Building a Common Core–based curriculum: Mapping with focus and fidelity.* Bloomington, IN: Solution Tree Press.

U.S. Department of Education. (2004). *Teaching children with attention deficit hyperactivity disorder: Instructional strategies and practices.* Accessed at www.ed.gov/teachers/needs/speced/adhd/adhd-resource-pt2.doc on October 3, 2017.

VanDerHeyden, A. M., Witt, J. C., & Gilbertson, D. (2007). Multiyear evaluation of the effects of a response to intervention (RTI) model on identification of children for special education. *Journal of School Psychology, 45*(2), 225–256.

Varnham, S. (2005). Seeing things differently: Restorative justice and school discipline. *Education and the Law, 17*(3), 87–104.

Vohs, K. D., & Baumeister, R. F. (Eds.). (2011). *Handbook of self-regulation: Research, theory, and applications* (2nd ed.). New York: Guilford Press.

Vygotsky, L. S. (1978). *Mind in society: The development of higher psychological processes.* Cambridge, MA: Harvard University Press.

Walker, H. M. (1997). *The acting-out child: Coping with classroom disruption* (2nd ed.). Longmont, CO: Sopris West.

Walker, H. M., Colvin, G., & Ramsey, E. (1995). *Antisocial behavior in school: Strategies and best practices.* Pacific Grove, CA: Brooks/Cole.

Walker, H. M., & Walker, J. E. (1991). *Coping with noncompliance in the classroom: A positive approach for teachers.* Austin, TX: Pro-Ed.

Walton, G. M., & Cohen, G. L. (2007). A question of belonging: Race, social fit, and achievement. *Journal of Personality and Social Psychology, 92*(1), 82–96.

Walton, G. M., & Cohen, G. L. (2011). A brief social-belonging intervention improves academic and health outcomes of minority students. *Science, 331*(6023), 1447–1451.

Wang, M. C., Haertel, G. D., & Wahlberg, H. J. (1994). Synthesis of research: What helps students learn? *Educational Leadership, 51*(4), 74–79.

Waters, M. B., Lerman, D. C., & Hovanetz, A. N. (2009). Separate and combined effects of visual schedules and extinction plus differential reinforcement on problem behavior occasioned by transitions. *Journal of Applied Behavioral Analysis*, *42*(2), 309–313.

Way, S. M. (2011). School discipline and disruptive classroom behavior: The moderating effects of student perceptions. *The Sociological Quarterly*, *52*(3), 346–375.

Weber, C. (2015a). *Behavioral RTI*. Paper presented at the Catholic Educators' Conference, Vancouver, British Columbia, Canada.

Weber (2015b). Creating consistency and collective responsibility. In A. Buffum & M. Mattos (Eds.), *It's about time: Planning interventions and extensions in elementary school* (pp. 225–253). Bloomington, IN: Solution Tree Press.

Wentzel, K. R. (1997). Student motivation in middle school: The role of perceived pedagogical caring. *Journal of Educational Psychology*, *89*(3), 411–419.

Wiggins, G. P., McTighe, J., Kiernan, L. J., & Frost, F. (1998). *Understanding by design*. Alexandria, VA: Association for Supervision and Curriculum Development.

Wiliam, D. (2016). *Leadership for teacher learning: Creating a culture where all teachers improve so that all students succeed*. West Palm Beach, FL: Learning Sciences International.

Wright, J. (n.d.). *Behavioral interventions*. Accessed at www.interventioncentral.org/behavioral-intervention-modification on February 13, 2018.

Yair, G. (2000). Reforming motivation: How the structure of instruction affects students' learning experiences. *British Educational Research Journal*, *26*(2), 191–210.

Yeager, D. S., & Walton, G. M. (2011). Social-psychological interventions in education: They're not magic. *Review of Educational Research*, *81*(2), 267–301.

Zimmerman, B. J., Bandura, A., & Martinez-Pons, M. (1992). Self-motivation for academic attainment: The role of self-efficacy beliefs and personal goal setting. *American Educational Research Journal*, *29*(3), 663–676.

Index

A

academic behaviors
    defined, 6, 7, 8–9
    integrating, 49–50
academic skills, nurturing skills through, 55–56
ACT, 10
adapt, 84, 102–103
administrative support, 129–130
Ainsworth, L., 19
Anderson County High School (Kentucky), 30
Armed Forces Qualification Test, 12
assessments. *See* formative assessments
attendance, 86
attentiveness, 103–104, 110–112

B

behavioral intervention programs, types of, 98
behavioral RTI
    See also Tier 1; Tier 2; Tier 3
    commitment to, 16–19, 39
    for all students, 134–135
    preassessment survey, 17, 18
    screening students, 41–44
    steps of, 4–5
    Tier 1, focusing on, 36–39
behavioral skills
    content-specific, 31–32, 33
    defined, 6–9
    defining key, 28–31
    formative assessment of, 60–70
    identifying and prioritizing, 19–28
    importance of, 3, 9–13
    integrating, 49–50
    modeling and teaching, 44–51
    nurturing, 52–56
    teacher preparation for modeling and teaching, 39–40
behavior documentation forms (BDFs), 70, 71–72, 89
Behavior Support Plan (BSP), 165–170
believe in yourself, 80–81, 104
belong, 81, 105
Bloom, B., 51, 91
Brookings Institute, 12
Buffum, A., 3–4

C

check-in/check-out (CI/CO), 70, 76, 116–119
cognitive restructuring, 83
cognitive skills, 12
Cohen, G. L., 15, 35
Collaborative for Academic, Social, and Emotional Learning (CASEL), 9
collaborative learning, 46
collaborative teams, 87
college- and career-readiness skills, 10–11
communication, teacher, 40
community conferencing, 124
community service, 124
completion of tasks, 86, 105, 110–112
conferences, teacher-student, 62, 68, 69

Uniting Academic and Behavior Interventions
Austin Buffum, Mike Mattos, Chris Weber, and Tom Hierck
Ensure students acquire the academic skills, dispositions, and knowledge necessary for long-term success. Examine what effective academic and behavior supports look like for all learners. Explore a step-by-step process for determining, targeting, and observing academic and behavior interventions.
BKF595

Pyramid of Behavior Interventions
Tom Hierck, Charlie Coleman, and Chris Weber
Students thrive when educators hold high expectations for behavior as well as academics. This book shows how to use a three-tiered pyramid of behavior supports to create a school culture and classroom climates in which learning is primed to occur.
BKF532

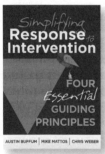

Simplifying Response to Intervention
Austin Buffum, Mike Mattos, and Chris Weber
The follow-up to *Pyramid Response to Intervention* advocates that effective RTI begins by asking the right questions to create a fundamentally effective learning environment for every student. Understand why paperwork-heavy, compliance-oriented, test-score-driven approaches fail. Then learn how to create an RTI model that works.
BKF506

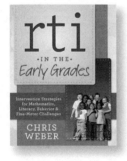

RTI in the Early Grades
Chris Weber
Explore why intervention and support for struggling students in the early grades are essential to student success. Teachers and support personnel will discover how to implement RTI-based supports in the early grades and learn what this looks like.
BKF572

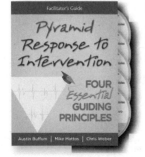

Pyramid Response to Intervention
Featuring Austin Buffum, Mike Mattos, and Chris Weber
Shift to a culture of collective responsibility, and ensure a path of opportunity and success for your students. Focusing on the four Cs vital to student achievement, this powerful four-part program will help you collect targeted information on each student's individual needs and guide you to build efficient team structures.
DVF057

Solution Tree | Press
a division of
Solution Tree

Visit SolutionTree.com or call 800.733.6786 to order.

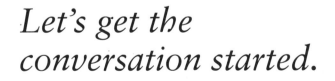